CELEBRATION

THE COLLECTION: VOLUME 2

CELEBRATION

RECIPES FROM COOPER'S HAWK FAMILY & FRIENDS

by Tim McEnery with Jeff Morgan
Photographs by Stephen Hamilton

Produced by

 Connected Dots Media

155 Montgomery Street, Suite 507
San Francisco, California 94104
www.connecteddotsmedia.com

Designed by Shawn Hazen
www.hazencreative.com

10 9 8 7 6 5 4 3 2 1

Cooper's Hawk Winery
430 E. Plainfield Road
Countryside, Illinois 60525
www.chwinery.com

Mediterranean Pot Roast with
Pappardelle Pasta
Ursula Korus
Page 146

CONTENTS

THE
RECIPES

THE COOPER'S HAWK STORY

This book was conceived as a gift for our wine club members. It's our way of saying THANK YOU. Our wine club members, our diners, and our dedicated, talented staff are all part of the Cooper's Hawk Community. Without them, Cooper's Hawk would not be what it is. I hope the pages that follow will give everyone an insider's view of how we came to be, how we work, and what makes Cooper's Hawk so special.

It's hard to believe how much has happened since we opened our first winery-restaurant back in October 2005. At that time, the winery was located on the lower level of the restaurant with viewing available only from the tasting room. It occupied a modest fraction of the total space. We were a pretty small crew in those early days. I was not only the winemaker but also ran the restaurant and oversaw the tasting room.

Back then, not everyone thought we could make Cooper's Hawk the kind of place it is today. In fact, twelve banks turned us down before we were finally able to get a loan. And my A-list of potential investors barely responded to my initial offering.

So you might wonder how such an inauspicious beginning grew into nine winery-restaurants with one of the largest wine clubs in America and a forty-five-thousand square-foot main winery that produces some fifty different wines each year. I honestly believe that simply having faith in the Cooper's Hawk concept was a key element in our early success. Perhaps equally important was our passion for wine and food. Ultimately—and possibly most important of all—everyone involved from the start was intent on building a community.

EARLY DAYS

I grew up in Orland Park, a suburb of Chicago. My aunt and uncle owned
a golf course and restaurant called Green Garden Country Club in nearby
Frankfort, and I started washing dishes at the restaurant when I was eleven.
By the time I was in high school, I was managing Green Garden's food
and beverage program. I would show up at the restaurant after school to
work for a few hours and leave my tie and jacket there for when I returned
later in the evening. I liked the restaurant's fast-paced environment and the
people I worked with.

After graduating from Purdue University with a major in restaurant and
hotel management, I returned to Green Garden, however I soon realized
that I needed to expand my horizons. I took a job at Prudential Securities
in Chicago as a financial advisor and learned a lot about managing money.
But after two years in the high-powered atmosphere of capital investment,
I missed the restaurant world and went back to Green Garden.

During my stint at Prudential, I met someone who would change the
course of my life. One evening, after a particularly bruising day at the office,
I stopped at a downtown Chicago bar to unwind with a drink and I met
Dana, who is now my wife. We were still dating after I left Prudential and
returned to Green Garden. I knew things were serious when Dana asked me
to go on a double date with her parents to a wine tasting at Lynfred Winery,
not far from Chicago in Roselle, and then to dinner at a nearby restaurant.

The winery was great, and though we had dinner plans, I remember
thinking that it was too bad that there wasn't a restaurant on the winery
premises. And that's how it all started.

The next day, I went online to look for restaurant-winery operations in
America and found only two, one in California and one in Michigan. I saw
an opportunity and began to create a business plan for Cooper's Hawk
that would take me two years to complete. Right away I knew that I would
need more experience with contemporary restaurant systems, standards,
and procedures than what I had learned at Green Garden, so I found a full-
time job at Aramark, one of the nation's largest food-service companies.
In my "spare time" I kept working on the Cooper's Hawk plan. To fill up my
week a bit more, I convinced the owner of Lynfred Winery, Fred Koehler,
to let me work there one day each week for some hands-on winery training.

Above: Tim at the crush.

Facing Page: The McEnery family: Tim, Dana, Ellie, and Keaton at home.

Basically I was working every free moment of the day and night. After two years, Dana had had enough. My eighty-plus-hour workweek wasn't conducive to family life. She told me I had to take the plunge and make Cooper's Hawk happen or we needed to get on with our lives and do something else. As usual, she was right.

I took my business plan to the Lettuce Entertain You consulting group, a large food-service organization based in Chicago. The meeting went well and I walked away feeling the concept could work. In retrospect, the meeting gave me the confidence I needed to continue working on the business plan.

I knew what I had to do. I left Aramark and was able to secure a full-time management position at Lynfred Winery. After sharing my idea with Fred Koehler, he agreed to give me a chance to manage his winery to see if it was a good fit for me. I wouldn't be here today if Fred and his family had not given me that opportunity. I was able to work on every aspect of running a winery. My first job wasn't glamorous. I had to count all of the wineglasses in the tasting room. Apparently, Fred suspected that his customers were keeping the winery's logo-embossed glasses as souvenirs. I thought to myself, "Of course they're keeping the glasses. Isn't that what we want them to do?" But I was there to learn, not teach, so I kept that notion to myself.

I also took a correspondence course from the University of California at Davis, the nation's premier school for winemaking. In all, the year proved to be invaluable. I learned how to make wine, and I also learned how to run a winery from the office to the bottling line. Now, with a good foundation in restaurant *and* winery management, I was ready to make my dream come true.

One thing I hadn't figured out yet was what to call the dream. We needed a name for the winery and restaurant. I went to the local library and got books on trees, rocks, geological terms, and birds. I was looking for something that spoke to me and had a kind of "Napa wine country" ring to it. Then I discovered a Cooper's hawk in the bird book. A beautiful, sleek-looking bird, it is native to North America and named after the nineteenth-century naturalist William Cooper. As I read about the hawk, I also found myself thinking about coopers, or barrel makers. That's when I knew we had a name.

So we had a name, a dream, and some professional skills, but we still didn't have any money to get started. Eventually I put together twenty-five

investors and secured a bank loan. Finding the start-up money was the hardest thing I had ever done in my life. But I soon discovered that finding a space to build a winery and restaurant would prove equally challenging.

FROM DREAM TO REALITY

In 2004, I came upon a project under way to construct a thirteen-thousand square-foot building in the Chicago suburb of Orland Park. The structure was designed to house multiple businesses, but because no space had yet been rented, the owner bet on me. The winery would operate on one side and the restaurant on the other. I would be the winemaker and the general manager.

First, we needed to create a working winery. We purchased tanks, pumps, and barrels and sourced grapes from vineyards in California and Washington. A lot of people don't realize that wineries aren't limited to estate grapes. We buy our grapes from growers in California, Oregon, Washington, New York, and Michigan, for example. Then at harvest, the handpicked grapes are shipped in refrigerated trucks to the winery, where they arrive in pristine condition.

The first Cooper's Hawk vintage in 2005 produced just over 1,800 cases of wine. While we were making wine, we were also constructing the restaurant and hiring the staff necessary to produce top-quality meals to be enjoyed with the wines. It was an intense time. By October 2005, Cooper's Hawk Winery & Restaurant was ready for its grand opening.

Running a winery or a restaurant is tough enough. But running both simultaneously was daunting and exhausting. Fortunately, in our second year, we were able to bring on a director of operations, Tom Roos. This gave me more time to focus on the Cooper's Hawk philosophy and our business.

Thanks to an incredibly supportive staff in both the winery and the restaurants, I can spend my time growing and evolving Cooper's Hawk. The goal is to provide an environment where almost anyone can come to taste the wine country without having to travel across the nation.

Our menu features both the new and the familiar. We make a broad range of varietals and styles to suit every preference. Each recipe in this book is paired with one of our wines and includes a wine profile to help you learn more about how it was made.

Above: In Naperville, the sun floods into the barrel room, which is available for private dining.

Top right: The main dining room at Arlington Heights.

By growing our company, we expand our community. Of course, our wine club is an essential part of that community, and it has become one of the largest wine clubs in America. Members not only receive wine on a monthly basis but also regularly attend intimate tasting and dinner events that feature guest chefs and sommeliers. Many of these dedicated professionals have contributed recipes to this book.

We even take club members on visits to European and American wine regions for an on-site taste of other wine communities. The trips encourage a special camaraderie and create new friendships, as well. With programs such as these, it's not surprising that our wine club continues to grow. It has become Cooper's Hawk's extended wine family.

My journey from adolescent dishwasher to winemaker and restaurateur has been an exciting one. In the pursuit of better wine service, I studied for and passed the examination for certified sommelier given by the renowned Court of Master Sommeliers. And I've tried to share this knowledge with all of our restaurant staff members. Today, Cooper's Hawk servers are given a five-day course in wine fundamentals to help them communicate clearly and effectively with our guests. Before service each day, there is a staff tasting in each restaurant to make sure everyone is familiar with the wine list.

The more I've learned, the more passionate I have become. That passion—along with a continuing quest for excellence—is what I hope to share with everyone in our Cooper's Hawk Community.

CHAPTER 1

MAKING WINE AT COOPER'S HAWK

Winemaking is an art that depends on three key elements: the quality of the grapes, their provenance, and the winemaker's skill. Without perfectly ripe grapes, it's impossible to make the finest wines. And without a highly skilled winemaker, it's not easy to coax the best quality from the grapes.

Provenance, however, is another story. Not every wine region is suited to growing the same kinds of wine grapes. Bordeaux, for example, favors Cabernet Sauvignon over Pinot Noir because the climate is more conducive to Cabernet. Burgundy, slightly cooler than Bordeaux, is more hospitable to Pinot Noir, which thrives at lower temperatures.

The same holds true for New World wines. In California, Oregon, and Washington, where Cooper's Hawk sources many of its grapes, variable soils and climate conditions make it possible to grow a wide variety of grapes. Top-notch Cabernet grapes may thrive in the Napa Valley or Washington's Columbia Valley, while first-rate Pinot Noir grapes can be found in the coastal areas of Oregon and California.

But the West Coast is not the only place to grow exceptional New World wine grapes. Canada, where Cooper's Hawk winemaker Rob Warren grew up and received a degree in oenology and viticulture from Brock University, is renowned for its ice wines. So is Michigan, where we source Vidal Blanc for our own Cooper's Hawk Ice Wine. And in New York we find Riesling and Concord grapes, the latter used to make our ever-popular Cooper's Hawk Sweet Red.

Above and Previous Page: Our grapes
come from great vineyards in California,
Oregon, Washington, and Michigan.
This one is in Napa Valley.

From the very beginning, I sourced grapes from many well-known New World wine regions to suit the winery's needs. The grapes were all hand-picked and shipped cold in refrigerated trucks directly from the vineyards to the winery in Illinois. It's a tradition that has been maintained by winemaker Rob Warren. The trick is to stay in regular contact with all of our grape growers throughout the growing season. That's how we know what is going on in the vineyards and when it is best to harvest. Picking at the optimal time is critical, so we work closely with our viticultural partners to make sure that only the finest grapes arrive at our winery in the fall.

THE HARVEST

In the northern hemisphere, the annual grape harvest typically begins in late August and stretches through October or November, depending on the vintage and the location. White grapes, except those used for ice wines or late-harvested dessert wines, tend to ripen before red grapes. So the first part of our harvest is primarily focused on whites and the second half on red wines.

Cooper's Hawk operates in essentially the same manner as any state-of-the-art winery in California or Washington, for example. The handpicked grapes arrive in the half-ton picking bins filled in the vineyards of origin. And because they are shipped very cold and sometimes arrive in as little time as two or three days from the West Coast and within hours from, say, Michigan, the grapes reach us in perfect condition. It's almost as if the vine-yards are located right outside our winery door!

FERMENTATION

Some white grapes are whole cluster pressed. That means that entire clusters are slowly pressed to extract the pure, clear juice. The juice travels from the press to tanks, where solids are allowed to settle out of the solution naturally for a day or so. Then the juice is transferred to fermentation tanks or barrels, depending on what kind of fermentation our winemaker desires.

Barrel fermentation of white wines is a time-honored method used most often for Chardonnay. It allows for the *best* integration of oak and produces wines of great elegance and complexity, such as our Lux Chardonnay. By contrast, tank fermentation tends to highlight fruitiness and may be the better choice for wines such as Riesling and Sauvignon Blanc.

Red grapes undergo a somewhat different procedure from white. As with white grapes, we receive the red grape clusters from the vineyards, but we mechanically remove the grapes from the stems using a destemmer. The whole berries are then crushed ever so slightly, which allows the juice to start slowly seeping out. As this occurs, the red grapes and juice are transferred to tanks for fermentation.

Interestingly, red wine grapes have white juice. In order for the wine to turn red, the juice must remain in contact with the red skins throughout fermentation. During this time, the pigment from the skins leeches out to deliver color, flavor, and tannin to the wine. This process takes two to four weeks, depending on how much natural sugar is in the grapes and how viable the fermentation yeasts are. When the wines go dry (that is, when all of the natural grape sugar has been consumed by yeast and transformed to alcohol), the wines are carefully transferred to barrels for aging.

Left: The crush begins immediately when the grapes arrive.

Below: Winemaker Rob Warren oversees the destemming process while Tim samples the juice.

Wine ages in the barrel and is tasted
regularly by Cooper's Hawk winemaker
Rob Warren.

Pennsylvania Oak

TH

M+

3Y

COOPER'S HAWK
WINERY & RESTAURANT

10MRKF
FILLED 11-30-10
SO₂ 2Tab 01-19-11
TOPPED 3-25-11
SO₂ 5/26/11
SO₂ 6-11-11
SO₂ 10-7-11

10-058

Barrel aging allows coarse tannins to soften and also gives the wines time to subtly integrate spicy, sweet oak into their flavor profile. Oak has long been used to highlight or enhance wine much in the same way that salt and pepper can enhance food. The trick, of course, is not to overdo it! Too much of a good thing is never a recipe for success.

SWEET WINES

Not all of our wines are fermented dry. Grapes picked for Cooper's Hawk Moscato and Ice Wine, for example, are harvested at such high levels of ripeness that it would be impossible to ferment all of the natural sugars. (Yeasts just give up after a certain point.) We let these sweet wines ferment until they are only partially dry, leaving natural residual sugar preserved.

The resulting wines may have varying levels of sweetness. Some, like our Riesling and Gewürztraminer, may be only slightly sweet. They can easily pair with both savory dishes and some desserts. Others, however, like our Moscato or Nightjar, which is a Port-style wine, are much sweeter. They are best appreciated on their own or with equally sweet foods.

BLENDING

Sometimes we make wines from only one grape variety, but we often follow the time-honored method of blending varietals, as well. In the latter case, the philosophy is that the sum will be greater than the parts.

In Bordeaux, for example, it is common to blend local varietals such as Cabernet Sauvignon, Cabernet Franc, Merlot, Malbec, and Petit Verdot. Our Lux Meritage is made in this style and gives our winemaker the opportunity to make the best of the best of each vintage.

Winemaking can take all sorts of imaginative turns, however, and we reserve the right to be as creative as possible. Sometimes this means making blends that are not as traditional as Lux Meritage. Cooper's Hawk Cabernet-Zinfandel blend may be at the top of the list in this department, with its fruity, jammy Zinfandel notes framed by classically structured Cabernet Sauvignon. In any case, the goal is always the same: to make the best possible wine.

COOPER'S HAWK WINE PORTFOLIO

To this end, we strive to bring out the best from what Mother Nature gives us. Our winemaker harvests the essence of the grape and turns it into a fabulous beverage for us to enjoy with a meal.

Numerous grape varieties, flavors, and styles exist, and we try to explore as many as possible. Because we offer such a diverse menu in our restaurants, we believe that every dish served should have an appropriate wine for pairing (see Pairing Food and Wine, page 33).

Of course, we don't all share the same tastes. But we want to make sure that everyone who comes to Cooper's Hawk can find a wine that he or she finds appealing. Who says you can't please all of the people all of the time? We aim to please, and we are grateful to hear from our customers that we are doing a good job. It is our pleasure to strive to exceed each customer's expectations every day.

That's why we make some fifty different wines today. It's a far cry from the early days back in 2005. We started with 1,812 cases of wine that first year and made only thirty-two varietals. Now, we've grown to about 120,000 cases and fifty varietals and special blends. It is gratifying to know that each day we host a diverse community of individuals who understand that quality of life is reflected in the quality of what we eat and what we drink.

Cooper's Hawk produces more than 50 varietals each year.

Top Sirloin with Masala Rub, Shiitake
Mushroom Risotto, and Broccolini
Evan Goldstein
Page 159

CHAPTER 2

PAIRING FOOD AND WINE

It's no wonder that wine and food go well together. A glass of wine refreshes the palate and leaves us ready for another bite of whatever we are eating. In addition, wine's natural acidity balances the natural oils and fats in the foods we eat. Simply stated, food and wine are a perfect match.

Not every wine pairs well with every dish, however. Some wines have an affinity for certain foods but not for others. The good news is that it's not hard to figure out what wines go best with various dishes. All you need are a few basic guidelines and you'll be pairing food and wine with the skill of a professional sommelier.

THE ELEMENTS OF STYLE

Nearly everyone has heard that white wines should be drunk with fish and red wines pair best with meats. It's not a bad principle, but we wouldn't call it gospel either. In fact, many whites and reds break the rule.

The key to pairing food and wine is simpler than most people think. It comes down to just one basic concept: similarly styled food and wine pair well together. What is meant by *styled*? Basically, *style* describes wine and food "personality." Is a wine full bodied, lush textured, and rich? Or is it light bodied, bright, and crisp? The same definitions can apply to what we eat. Is your steak rich and robust? Is your salad light and refreshing?

If you can describe what's on your plate, you can easily decide on what kind of wine to drink with dinner. It just so happens that white wines tend to be lighter bodied than red wines, which are usually full bodied. Not all white

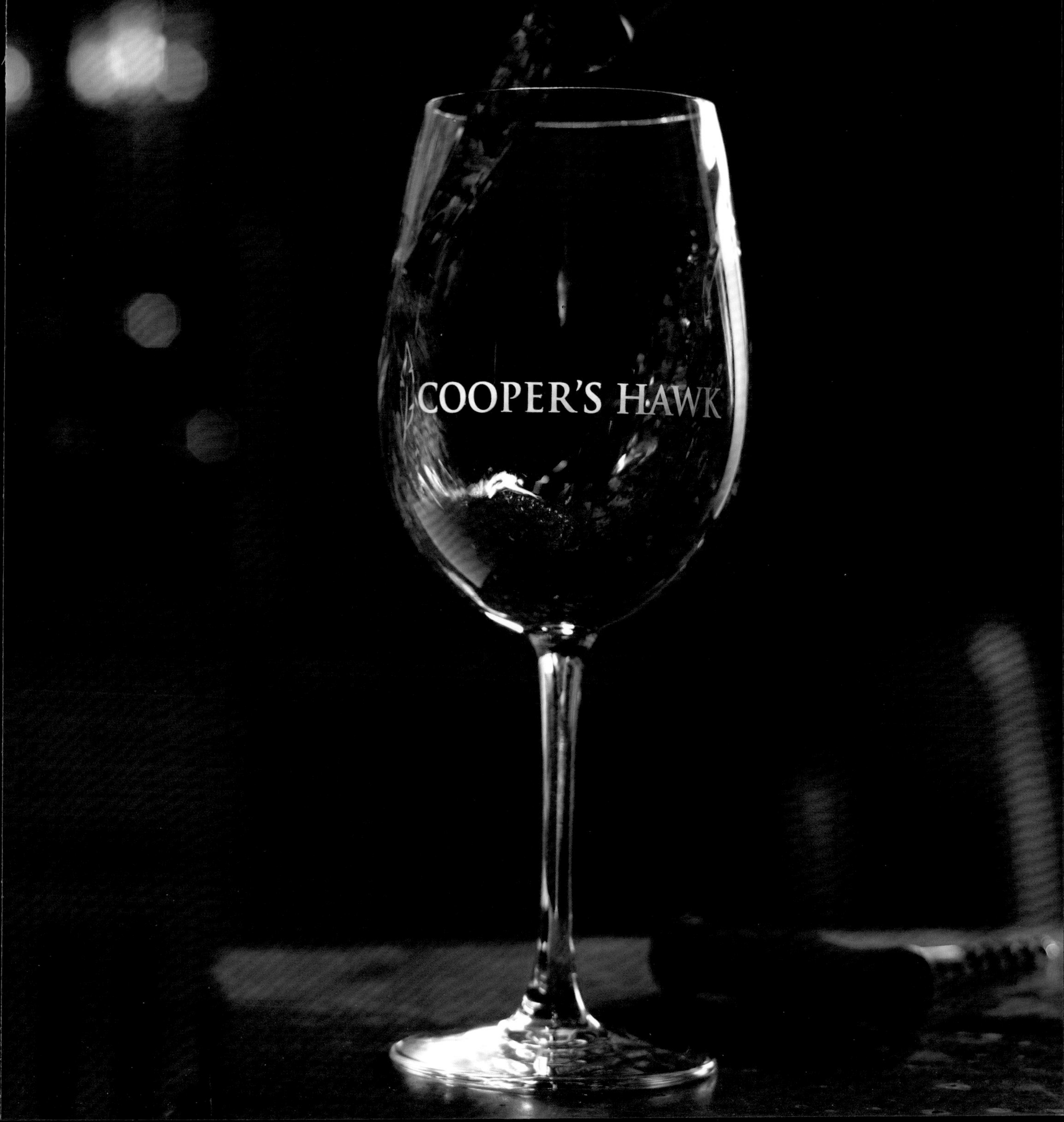
COOPER'S HAWK

wines are created equal, however. Some are lighter and others are richer. The same thing applies to red wines.

The best way to determine a wine's style is to taste it. Unfortunately, you can't always do that before you choose a wine in a restaurant or to drink at home. That's why it helps to have a general idea of how various white wines and red wines taste. This isn't rocket science, and an educated guess is often a good one! You'll find more information to help you select the best wines to pair with meals in the discussion of wine varietals and their style later in this chapter (see page 38).

COMPLEMENTARY AND CONTRASTING PAIRINGS

Before I go into more detail about wine varietals, I want to focus on the concept of style. Essentially, two kinds of food and wine pairings exist: complementary and contrasting. Similarly styled food and wine pairings are called complementary; a classic complementary pairing would be a full-bodied Cabernet Sauvignon enjoyed with a big, rich steak. This is the most common type of pairing. Other complementary pairings might include a bright, tangy Sauvignon Blanc with scallop seviche (page 62) or a medium-bodied Pinot Noir with an herbed chicken (page 139).

Food and wine that come from opposite ends of the stylistic spectrum yet still work well together is a contrasting pairing. These marriages are less prevalent in our daily dining but are nonetheless notable. Caviar and Champagne are a famously contrasting pairing. The wine's tangy, light bubbles and crisp acidity provide a counterweight to the salty richness of the fish eggs that somehow works.

THE PERFECT MATCH

So how do we know what wine to choose for that perfect dinner match? More often than not, complementary pairings work best. But there is no one "perfect" pairing for any dish. Think less about a wine's color and more about its style. Then think about the style of the dish you're eating. Key words to keep in mind are light, fresh, full, rich, heavy, creamy, sweet, and dry. (Sweet wines are best with sweet foods, and dry wines—those without sweetness—pair better with savory foods.)

What you drink will affect the way you experience your meal. But there is so much middle ground that it's easier than not to make the "right" choices.

Dishes that are not particularly light textured or rich will probably fall somewhere in between, where medium-bodied wines also abound. The pairing choices are legion. Perhaps most important, whatever you enjoy drinking and eating is the "right choice." Ultimately, you are your own best arbiter of good taste.

WINE'S FLAVORS

You'll notice that I haven't even mentioned flavor yet. Flavor is important, of course, but for the purpose of making pairing decisions, flavor is not a key component in the same way style is. Still, the myriad of flavors in a glass of wine can be quite noteworthy. And they can play a role in making pairings more or less successful.

Where do the flavors in wine come from? Grapes (and all fruits and vegetables) are blessed with a complex array of aromatic and flavor compounds known as essential oils. The concentration of these compounds will determine whether a lemon tastes like a lemon or a cherry tastes like a cherry. Grapes have a wonderfully high and varied collection of these compounds, also known as terpenes and esters. When grape juice is fermented, the resulting alcohol acts to carry these flavors to your palate.

Ripe grapes can also harbor flavors found in many other fruits. White grapes tend to carry flavors found in light-colored fruits, such as lemons, melons, and peaches. Red grapes serve up red fruit flavors, like cherries, blackberries, and plums. Both red and white grapes may also display herbal qualities reminiscent of sage, thyme, fresh-mowed grass, or mint. This diversity of flavor is what makes wine possibly the most interesting beverage on the planet.

BASIC WINE VARIETALS AND THEIR STYLE

In the United States, wines are usually referred to by their varietal. That is, a wine is described by the grape variety from which it is made. Chardonnay, for example, is a grape as well as a wine. So is Cabernet Sauvignon. There are hundreds of grape varieties, but only a relatively small number are commonly used in winemaking today.

Wines can also be made from a blend of varietals. This is a time-honored practice that dates back to the very beginnings of winemaking. However, a wine can only be labeled with the name of the varietal if that varietal makes up at least 75 percent of the blend. What follows is a list of varietals made

at Cooper's Hawk accompanied by descriptions to help define the styles in which they are commonly made. The information is general but can be helpful when deciding on pairing food and wine.

WHITE WINES

Chardonnay: America's most popular white wine, Chardonnay can be made in many different styles, from rich, toasty, and full bodied to lean and light bodied. Some of these differences are due to climate, soil, and other vineyard elements that affect the ripening process. Other stylistic distinctions can be attributed to winemaking techniques. A barrel-fermented Chardonnay, for example, is typically much richer and fuller bodied than one that is tank fermented. In general, look among all Chardonnays for an elegant and refreshing wine that can show off pretty apple, pear, and citrus flavors. Barrel-fermented versions will also boast hints of toast and butterscotch. Unoaked Chardonnays lean toward a light-bodied citrus, minerally profile.

Sauvignon Blanc: Best known for its bracing acidity, this lively—almost feisty—varietal is loaded with zippy lemony flavors. Grapefruit and passion fruit also often come to mind. Sauvignon Blanc is typically made in a fresh, light style, with many examples noteworthy for their distinctively "grassy" aromas that recall freshly cut hay. Melon and fig notes can be discerned in very ripe examples of this rising star among varietals.

Pinot Gris: Also referred to by its Italian name, Pinot Grigio, this wine is more restrained and subtly perfumed than either Chardonnay or Sauvignon Blanc. It typically serves up terrific acidity, which gives it great structure. On the palate it offers a pleasing array of flavors, ranging from stone fruit, such as nectarine and peach, to steely mineral notes.

Riesling: Known in Germany as the king of grapes, Riesling is marked by bright acidity and lovely peach and honey flavors. To offset its crispness, the varietal is often made in a sweet or semisweet style. But it doesn't have to be. Dry Riesling will offer the same fruit flavors without the sweetness.

Gewürztraminer: Another grape of German origin, classic Gewürztraminer is often distinguished by a spiciness redolent of cloves, ginger, and nutmeg. In fact, *Gewürz* means "spice" in German. Look for hints of lychee nut and stone fruit as well in this seductive and exotic varietal. As with Riesling, Gewürztraminer can be made in sweet or dry styles.

Viognier: Not long ago, this varietal—native to the Rhône Valley in France—was rarely seen outside the rarefied world of wine connoisseurs. Today, Viognier vines have been transplanted to America. The resulting wines are redolent of stone fruit and spice and often richly textured. They make a fine alternative to Chardonnay.

Moscato: Also known as Muscat and commonly grown in northern Italy and southern France, this fruit-forward varietal serves up hints of peaches and apricots. It is commonly made into a sweet sparkling wine in Italy and a sweet still wine in France. Sweet or dry, Moscato offers a fruity vibrancy rarely found in other white varietals.

ROSÉS

Unlike white wines and red wines, rosés are not usually referred to by their varietals. The word *rosé* comes from the French word for "pink" and simply describes the wine's color.

The best-known and most widely drunk rosés in America are White Zinfandels made from red Zinfandel grapes. These wines are produced in a somewhat sweet style that differentiates them from the new wave of dry (not sweet) rosés currently and increasingly embraced by many wine lovers.

Dry rosés are not quite red and not quite white, but instead somewhere in between. They have the firm acidity found in most white wines, which is why they are drunk chilled. But they also harbor red fruit flavors that remind us of strawberries, raspberries, and cherries.

RED WINES

Cabernet Sauvignon: Full bodied and richly textured, Cabernet Sauvignon shows off a broad spectrum of flavors: blackberry, cassis, plum, black cherry, tea, licorice, and even chocolate. It is often blessed with herbal notes such as thyme and sage and is generally framed in toasty oak, which comes from the barrels used to age it.

Merlot: Similar to Cabernet Sauvignon, Merlot is somewhat less robust or full bodied on the palate. It is blessed with fruit flavors comparable to those found in Cabernet, but it can display softer texture on the palate. As a result, Merlot is sometimes considered easier to drink when younger than Cabernet.

Serving Wine

Here are a few simple tips to coax the most out of a bottle of good wine.

GLASSWARE

The shape of your glass does make a difference. So does its size. But there is no "best" shape or size, despite what some wineglass manufacturers might have us believe. Custom has dictated shape in various parts of the world. And many people do prefer a larger glass for red wines. But what really counts is having a glass large enough to conserve aromatics with a pour that fills one-third to one-half the glass. Twelve to sixteen ounces is an excellent size for an all-purpose wineglass. The sides should be concave and the edges thin to promote a seamless journey from the glass to your palate.

DECANTING

Transferring wine from a bottle to a decanter, though not a requirement, can serve a useful purpose. For example, it can aerate young reds, which can soften tannins and reveal hidden aromas and flavors. White wines can also benefit from aeration, though they are less commonly decanted.

Older wines may have sediments that have fallen out of solution and collected at the bottom of the bottle. In this case, decanting allows you to separate the wine from the solids, which may be bitter or otherwise unpleasant.

We often use decanters at our restaurants. They provide both a beautiful visual framework and a way to highlight the flavors in the bottle.

TEMPERATURE

Temperature does matter. A wine that is too cold will be less flavorful. And a wine that is too warm will appear to be unbalanced and even hot on the tongue. There is no perfect temperature for wine. Ideally, white wines should be enjoyed at around 50°F and red wines are excellent at around 65°F. But many of us don't have a thermometer on hand to measure temperature. In general, remove your white wines and rosés from the refrigerator about 10 minutes before drinking them. If your home is warmer than 70°F, you might want to chill down your red wines for 10 minutes in the refrigerator prior to opening.

Pinot Noir: Highly versatile when it comes to food and wine pairing, Pinot Noir is more light bodied than many other reds. Nonetheless, it is blessed with good structure and layers of flavor. At its core, look for pretty cherry notes. They'll be backed by hints of spice, toast, and herbs. Well-made Pinot Noir is extremely elegant and refined.

Malbec: This varietal hails from Bordeaux, where it is one of the five famous core varietals that make up many classic Bordeaux red blends. Its adopted home in Argentina has also become a bellwether for quality, where Malbec stands on its own as a varietal. Malbec's larger leaves and clusters differentiate it from other red Bordeaux grape varieties. A cherry-like quality and soft, round tannins make this easy-drinking wine a perfect match for many types of dishes, including red meats, poultry, and seafood.

Wine in the Cooper's Hawk Tasting
Room in Naperville.

Barbera: This varietal hails originally from northern Italy, where it makes some of that country's most renowned red wines. The grape is known for its bright acidity (a bit like Pinot Noir) and desirable cherry and berry flavors. It makes a medium-bodied wine recognized as a versatile varietal for pairing with many kinds of food.

Sangiovese: In Tuscany, Sangiovese reigns supreme. Blessed with bright acidity and the ability to produce complex, age-worthy flavors, Sangiovese is a wine lover's red. Many of Italy's most famous wines have been produced with this grape. But it is not nearly as commonly planted in the United States as Cabernet Sauvignon and Pinot Noir.

Zinfandel: Best known in California, where it has been grown successfully since the mid-1800s, Zinfandel is known for its spicy, fruity appeal. The wine is often redolent of strawberries, raspberries, blackberries, and cherries, along with hints of vanilla, cinnamon, and other spices. When made with very ripe grapes, it can show a "jammy" quality.

Syrah: Sometimes also referred to by its Australian moniker, Shiraz, Syrah is often blessed with earthy overtones. In this case, "earthy" is a good thing. The wine can display aromas that remind us of the smells of the forest, like mushrooms and fallen leaves. But Syrah also has a vibrant, fruity component with hints of blackberry and black cherry combined with spicy, herbal notes.

Petite Sirah: This is not Syrah, but instead a distinct varietal that was created in France more than a century ago by crossing Syrah grapes with an obscure varietal called Peloursin. Petite Sirah didn't go far in France, but it has thrived in America, particularly in California. Although it is not widely planted today, it is still enjoyed by many for its deep, dark color and rich, plush plum, blackberry, and smoke flavors.

Tempranillo: Most commonly found in the Rioja region of Spain, Tempranillo has long been among the most popular wine grapes in that country. Here in America, it is not planted nearly as widely as more popular grapes such as Cabernet Sauvignon and Pinot Noir. But it has a small, dedicated following of aficionados who appreciate its bright acidity, firm tannins, and spicy red fruit flavors.

Pizza Agliarulo
Jonathan Goldsmith
Page 100

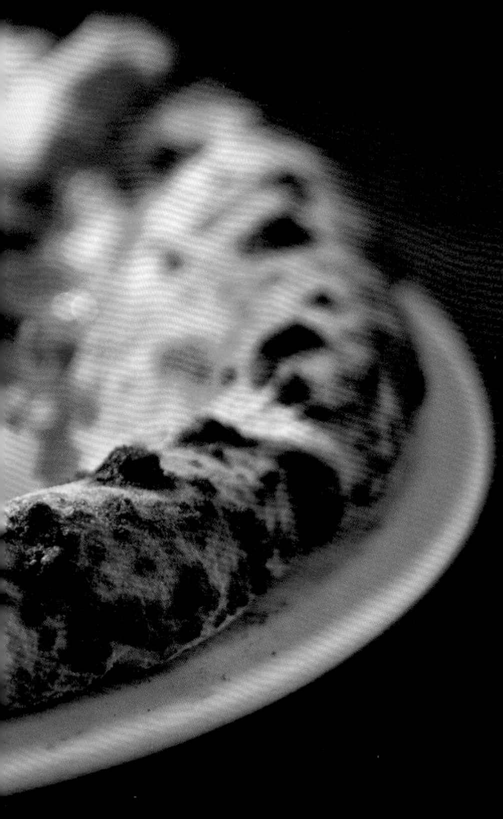

CHAPTER 3

RECIPES AND WINE PROFILES

Friends and family are the heart of Cooper's Hawk. They are at the center of life's celebrations.

A number of recipes featured in this book were created by members of the Cooper's Hawk team, including chef Matt McMillin, chef José Esparza, winemaker Rob Warren, and my wife, Dana, and I. But most of the recipes have been generously contributed by friends of Cooper's Hawk. They include nationally renowned chefs, sommeliers, and other food and wine professionals who have graciously shared their knowledge and talent in many ways. Some have cooked at special Cooper's Hawk Wine Club events; others have worked closely with us to help make the Cooper's Hawk experience—both in the restaurants and in your wineglass—the best that it can be.

All of the recipes include biographical information about the contributors, and every dish is paired with a different Cooper's Hawk wine. I hope that you will enjoy reading about our friends and our wines, and that you'll try making some of these excellent recipes. All of them have been tested in a home kitchen and as a result are easy to prepare.

Bon appétit!

Bridget Albert
DIRECTOR OF MIXOLOGY
SOUTHERN WINE & SPIRITS, BOLINGBROOK, ILLINOIS

VINE RIPE COCKTAIL

Here's a classy cocktail brought to us by Bridget Albert, Master Mixologist. Bridget honed her skills working behind the bar at the illustrious Bellagio resort in Las Vegas. She currently designs cocktail programs for many of the finest restaurants in Illinois and has had significant influence on our offerings at Cooper's Hawk. Bridget is also the coauthor of *Market-Fresh Mixology* (Surrey Books, 2008).

This cocktail has just the right amount of fresh fruit, sweetness, and zippy bubbles, all blended neatly with our distinctive rhubarb wine, then chilled and served in a long-stemmed martini glass.

The drink is easy to make, but it helps to have a cocktail shaker and strainer. You'll also need to prepare it in three stages: make the simple syrup first, then marinate your "drunken berries," and finally mix the drink. Remember to go easy on the ginger ale, too. It's really just a garnish; use too much and you'll lose the flavor of the wine.

And since only a small amount of wine is used here, enjoy the rest of the bottle with a main course, such as Dana's Parmesan-Crusted Chicken (page 131).

VINE RIPE COCKTAIL

Simple Syrup

1 cup water

1 cup sugar

Drunken Berries

½ pint (about 1 cup) raspberries

¼ cup Grand Marnier

¼ cup simple syrup (above)

Cocktail

Ice cubes

2½ ounces Cooper's Hawk Rhubarb
  Wine

1 ounce white rum

Juice of 1 lemon wedge

½ ounce juice from drunken berries
  (above)

1 or 2 splashes ginger ale

2 teaspoons drunken berries (above)

To make the simple syrup, in a small saucepan, bring the water and sugar to a boil over high heat, stirring occasionally until the sugar has dissolved, about 4 minutes. Remove from the heat and let cool to room temperature before using. The syrup will keep in an airtight container in the refrigerator for up to 1 week.

To prepare the drunken berries, in a small bowl, mix together all of the ingredients. Cover and refrigerate for at least 1 hour or up to 24 hours. (Only a small amount of the berries will be used for each cocktail. Reserve the remainder for another use.)

To make the cocktail, half fill a cocktail shaker with ice. Add the wine, rum, lemon juice, and berry juice, cover, and shake vigorously. Strain into a long-stemmed martini glass. Top with the ginger ale, stir, and garnish with the drunken berries.

MAKES 1 DRINK

Cooper's Hawk Rhubarb Wine

Cooper's Hawk winemaker Rob Warren says that rhubarb is similar to grapes in its chemical structure and thus lends itself to winemaking. This wine is pale pink, similar to a rosé. On the palate, it is fresh and lively, serving up a lovely spiced rhubarb pie note on the finish. With just a hint of sweetness, our rhubarb wine offers an excellent beverage option before or during a meal.

UNCOMMON PARSLEY PESTO AND GOAT CHEESE WHIP WITH HOMEMADE POTATO CHIPS

Helen and Michael Cameron are the proprietors of distinctly uncommon ground: a twenty-five-hundred square-foot certified organic rooftop farm thirty feet above Devon Avenue on the north side of Chicago. They and other farmers practicing sustainable, organic agriculture provide ingredients for the Camerons' community-based, eponymous restaurants in the Lakeview and Edgewater areas of Chicago. Both Uncommon Ground restaurants advocate the principles of local sustainably and organically produced food. The Green Restaurant Association in Boston has awarded them a four-star certification for their efforts.

The Camerons offer us a terrific dish to kick off a dinner party. A glass of Cooper's Hawk Blanc de Blanc serves up a sparkling aperitif to accompany this appealing appetizer. The whip has a refreshing herbal quality couched in a creamy blend of cheeses.

Remember to let the potato chips turn golden brown before removing them from the hot oil. If they are undercooked, they won't be crisp enough to scoop up the whip effectively.

UNCOMMON PARSLEY PESTO AND GOAT CHEESE WHIP WITH HOMEMADE POTATO CHIPS

4 large russet potatoes (about 2½ pounds), unpeeled

1 cup extra virgin olive oil

2 cups firmly packed fresh Italian parsley leaves

3 cloves garlic, minced

1 cup grated pecorino cheese

¾ cup pine nuts, toasted (see page 183)

Salt

5 ounces Capriole or other high-quality fresh soft goat cheese, at room temperature

5 ounces Neufchâtel or other high-quality cream cheese, at room temperature

½ cup half-and-half

Canola oil for deep-frying

Using a mandoline or a food processor, slice the potatoes crosswise as thinly as possible. If necessary, cut the potatoes in half lengthwise so they fit into the feeder tube of the processor. Place the slices in a large nonreactive bowl and add cold water to cover. Let soak for 2 hours, changing the water twice.

While the potatoes are soaking, prepare the whip. To make the pesto, using a blender or food processor, combine the olive oil, parsley, and garlic and purée until smooth. Add the pecorino cheese and pine nuts and continue to purée. The consistency will be thick but smooth. Season to taste with salt.

In a medium bowl, combine the pesto, goat cheese, and Neufchâtel cheese. Using an electric mixer, beat together the ingredients, starting on low speed and slowly increasing the speed to medium as the consistency allows. Use a rubber spatula to scrape down the sides of the bowl as needed and continue to beat until the mixture is smooth. Slowly add the half-and-half and continue to beat until all of the ingredients are well blended, about 30 seconds. Set the whip aside while you fry the potatoes, or cover and refrigerate until ready to use. It will keep for up to 3 days. (If refrigerating, remove the whip from the refrigerator 30 minutes prior to serving.)

Pour the canola oil to a depth of 1 inch into a large, high-sided skillet and heat over high heat.

Drain the potatoes in a colander. Pat the slices dry on paper towels, removing as much of the moisture as possible. When the oil in the pan starts to shimmer, test it with a potato slice. If the slice sizzles and creates tiny bubbles right away, the oil is ready.

Working in small batches, carefully place the potato slices in the hot oil, separating the slices occasionally with metal tongs to prevent them from sticking together. Be careful not to overfill the pan or the potatoes will not cook evenly. Cook until crisp and golden brown, about 10 minutes. (Do not undercook the chips or they won't be crisp enough for scooping the whip.) Using a slotted metal spatula or tongs, remove the chips from the oil and drain on paper towels. Repeat with the remaining potato slices. Season the chips with salt to taste.

Serve the chips warm or at room temperature with the whip.

SERVES 6 TO 8 AS AN APPETIZER

WINE PROFILE

Cooper's Hawk Blanc de Blanc Sparkling Wine

Our celebratory sparkling wine is made from 100 percent Chardonnay grapes. Following President Obama's election in 2008, the wine was selected by the Illinois delegation for its inaugural ball. I personally drove our Blanc de Blanc to Washington for the occasion!

We use the same tried-and-true methods created by our French colleagues in Champagne to produce a wine of uncommon freshness and finesse. Tiny bubbles add a lightness to the palate while transporting flavors that range from citrus and green apple to hints of toast and almonds. Enjoy this wine with almost any appetizer or light-bodied dish. Or drink it on its own for the perfect aperitif.

ASPARAGUS WITH MANCHEGO CHEESE

This recipe, graciously provided by Art Smith, is a perfect example of simple flavors combining to create a rich, complex dish. Art fell in love with asparagus when his mother began feeding him tiny morsels of the grassy spears as a baby. Many years later, during a visit to Spain, he discovered Manchego cheese, a buttery, slightly piquant aged sheep's milk cheese, and found that it paired beautifully with asparagus.

Art is the executive chef and co-owner of Table Fifty-Two in his hometown of Chicago; Art and Soul in Washington, D.C.; Southern Art and Bourbon Bar in Atlanta, Georgia; and LYFE Kitchen in Palo Alto, California. His new Italian-American eatery, Joanne's, is slated to open soon in Manhattan.

Art's passions and talents extend beyond the kitchen. He is the founder of Common Threads, an organization that educates children about different cultures through food and art, and has authored two cookbooks: *Back to the Table* and *Kitchen Life*. He has appeared on *Top Chef* and other leading television shows and for ten years held the prestigious position of personal chef to Oprah Winfrey.

ASPARAGUS WITH MANCHEGO CHEESE

1 tablespoon extra virgin olive oil,
   plus more for the baking dish
1 loaf (1 pound) French bread, cut
   into small cubes
1 onion, diced
2 cups halved cherry or grape
   tomatoes
3½ cups diagonally cut asparagus
   (½-inch pieces)
8 eggs
1 cup whole milk
½ cup grated Parmesan cheese
   (about 2 ounces)
1 teaspoon kosher salt
Freshly ground black pepper
1 cup shredded Manchego cheese

Preheat the oven to 350°F. Lightly grease a 13-by-9-inch baking dish with olive oil. Spread the bread cubes in a single layer in the prepared baking dish and set aside.

In a large skillet, heat the olive oil over medium heat. Add the onion and sauté until translucent, about 3 minutes. Add the tomatoes and asparagus and cook for 2 minutes longer. Pour the asparagus mixture evenly over the bread cubes.

In a bowl, whisk together the eggs, milk, Parmesan cheese, salt, and a few grinds of pepper until well blended. Pour the egg mixture evenly over the vegetable and bread cubes, then sprinkle the Manchego cheese evenly over the top.

Bake until the top is golden brown, 40 to 45 minutes. Serve immediately.

SERVES 6 TO 8 AS A SIDE DISH

Cooper's Hawk Chardonnay

This full-bodied, opulent chardonnay is an excellent companion to the rich, briny notes found in the Spanish Manchego cheese used to flavor this dish. The pronounced aromas of lemon zest, Golden Delicious apple, Asian pear, and acacia flower provide a fine contrast to the creamy, baked sheep's milk cheese and herbal asparagus aromas. It's a refreshing wine with hints of spice highlighting the fresh fruit finish.

Ron Edwards
MASTER SOMMELIER
CHARLEVOIX, MICHIGAN

SCALLOP SEVICHE

As one of only 184 wine experts in the world to have earned the esteemed title of Master Sommelier, Ron Edwards brings an incredible wealth of knowledge to his quarterly seminars at Cooper's Hawk. He sees himself as a "wine ambassador" who approaches training and consulting from the perspective of the consumer. His point of view has had a positive impact on shaping the service culture in our restaurants as a whole.

Ron's seviche is made with plump, sweet scallops "cooked" in lime juice—a fine match for the citrus flavors found in Cooper's Hawk Sauvignon Blanc. The presentation is as classy as it is colorful, with ivory scallops backed by a tableau of red and yellow peppers and shades of green from the avocado, onion, and jalapeño.

Seviche is easy to prepare. Just combine all of the ingredients and wait for an hour or so for the lime juice to do its work. Day boat sea scallops are large, tender scallops. This recipe will also work with smaller bay scallops, but you will need to measure them by weight (8 ounces), not by the number of scallops. Ron also notes that you can substitute just about any white-fleshed fish fillets for the scallops.

4 to 6 day boat sea scallops (about 8
  ounces), cut into ½-inch cubes
½ red pepper, finely diced
½ yellow pepper, finely diced
1 small jalapeño or serrano chile,
  seeded and very finely diced (about
  1½ tablespoons)
2 green onions, white and tender green
  parts only, thinly sliced
¼ cup minced fresh cilantro
1 clove garlic, minced
Juice of 2 limes (about ⅓ cup)
Salt
1 small, ripe avocado, halved, pitted,
  peeled, and diced
Freshly ground black pepper (optional)
1 lime, quartered

In a medium nonreactive bowl, combine the scallops, peppers, jalapeño chile, green onions, cilantro, and garlic. In a small bowl, stir together the lime juice and 1 teaspoon salt and pour over the scallop mixture. Mix all of the ingredients thoroughly. Cover and refrigerate for at least 1 hour or up to 2 hours. Do not marinate for too long or the fish will become mushy.

Just before serving, remove the bowl from the refrigerator and gently mix in the avocado. Taste and adjust the seasoning with more salt if needed and with pepper if desired.

Divide the seviche evenly among 4 large-stemmed martini glasses or small glass bowls. Garnish with a lime wedge on the rim or on the seviche itself.

SERVES 4

Cooper's Hawk Sauvignon Blanc

Sauvignon Blanc is a distinctive white grape that expresses itself in decidedly different ways depending on where it is grown. In cooler climates such as New Zealand or the Loire Valley of northern France, it can be marked by an extreme grassiness that comes from a natural chemical component in the grape. Somewhat warmer regions like Bordeaux and the Napa Valley tend to produce wines with a bit more opulence. In these areas, the grassiness is toned down somewhat and other flavors come to the fore. Cooper's Hawk Sauvignon Blanc is made from grapes grown in Napa Valley's Rutherford district. With crisp acidity, the wine shows classic varietal notes that include a solid grapefruit and lemon core framed with lovely hints of grass or fresh-cut hay.

Scallop Seviche, page 62

Shawn McClain
CHEF AND OWNER
GREEN ZEBRA RESTAURANT, CHICAGO, ILLINOIS

WHITE WINE–POACHED PEAR SALAD WITH FETA, TOASTED ALMONDS, AND CITRUS DRESSING

Wine-poached pears brighten up this refreshingly original salad contributed by chef Shawn McClain, who has created a temple of fine vegetarian cuisine at Green Zebra, which he opened in 2004. Shawn has received many honors for his creative and contemporary cooking, not the least of which was Chef of the Year from *Esquire* magazine in 2001.

In this recipe, spicy arugula is tempered by creamy feta cheese, while toasted almonds add a pleasing, crunchy finishing touch. The dish reveals a freshness and stunning purity of flavor that serves as a fine foil to our *Méthode Champenoise* sparkling wine.

2 cups dry white wine

½ cup fresh lemon juice, plus juice of 1 lemon

1 tablespoon coriander seeds

2 tablespoons fennel seeds

1 bay leaf

1 tablespoon black peppercorns

Salt

½ cup sugar

4 Bosc pears, halved, stemmed, peeled, and cored

Juice of ½ orange (about 2 tablespoons)

2 tablespoons extra virgin olive oil

Freshly ground black pepper

4 ounces arugula

4 ounces feta cheese, crumbled (about ½ cup)

¼ cup slivered blanched almonds, toasted (see page 183)

In a medium saucepan, combine 3 cups water, the wine, ½ cup lemon juice, coriander seeds, fennel seeds, bay leaf, peppercorns, 2 teaspoons salt, and the sugar and bring to a boil over high heat, stirring occasionally to dissolve the sugar. Reduce the heat to medium and simmer for 5 minutes. Add the pear halves, reduce the heat to medium-low, and cook until they can be easily pierced with a fork, 15 to 20 minutes.

Using a slotted spoon, transfer the pear halves to a large plate. Discard the poaching liquid. Let the pears cool to room temperature, then cover and refrigerate until well chilled, about 1 hour.

When the pears are ready, cut the halves lengthwise into ½-inch-wide strips and set aside.

To make the dressing, in a small glass bowl, whisk together the remaining juice of 1 lemon, the orange juice, and the olive oil. Season to taste with salt and pepper, mixing well.

To assemble the salad, in a large bowl, combine the arugula, cheese, and almonds. Add the dressing and toss to coat well. Divide the salad among individual plates. Divide the pear strips among the plates, arranging them on top of the salad. Garnish each serving with a grind or two of pepper and serve.

SERVES 4 TO 6

White Wine–Poached Pear Salad with Feta, Toasted Almonds, and Citrus Dressing, page 66

WINE PROFILE

Cooper's Hawk Méthode Champenoise Sparkling Wine

This richly textured bubbly is made using a technique created by our French colleagues in Champagne. It is blessed with tiny bubbles and mounds of flavor. Toasty, nutty notes lead the way, framing a bright, lemony core that refreshes to the very last drop. Our sparkling wine is delicious with almost any appetizer or light-bodied dish. Here, it pairs elegantly with a poached pear salad. But you can also drink *Méthode Champenoise* sparkler on its own as the perfect aperitif.

Fabio Viviani
CHEF AND OWNER
CAFÉ FIRENZE, MOORPARK, CALIFORNIA, AND
OSTERIA FIRENZE, LOS ANGELES, CALIFORNIA

BEEF AND BARLEY SOUP

Italian-born chef Fabio Viviani brings a wealth of culinary artistry to us from his roots in Italy and his professional experience on both sides of the Atlantic. He began his career at age twelve in a bakery in Florence, where he was born. Slowly he worked his way into the kitchens of several top restaurants, and by age sixteen, Fabio was sous-chef at Il Pallaio, a fast-paced trattoria in his hometown.

In 2006, at the age of twenty-seven, Fabio moved to the United States, where he has opened two restaurants in Southern California, Café Firenze in Moorpark and Osteria Firenze in Los Angeles. The young chef has also been seen by millions on television, where he was a finalist in season five of Bravo's *Top Chef*. He is among the friends of Cooper's Hawk who have graced our winery and restaurants with their talent and charisma.

This deceptively simple recipe is loaded with flavor and will warm you up on a cold winter night. Beef barley soup is a classic dish. But here, the addition of something as seemingly incongruous as four tiny cloves gives this version a special quality. The rich, full-bodied soup is a meal in itself, pairing beautifully with Cooper's Hawk Cabernet Sauvignon.

4 tablespoons extra virgin olive oil

1½ pounds boneless chuck roast, cut
  into 1-inch cubes and patted dry

1 onion, diced

3 cloves garlic, minced

2 large carrots, thinly sliced

2 celery stalks, thinly sliced

2 parsnips, peeled and thinly sliced

4 fresh thyme sprigs, about 4 inches
  long

1 bay leaf

4 whole cloves

1½ teaspoons salt

Freshly ground black pepper

2½ quarts homemade or store-bought
  low-sodium beef broth

½ cup pearl barley

¼ cup minced fresh Italian parsley

In a Dutch oven or large, heavy soup pot, heat 2 tablespoons of the olive oil over high heat. Working in batches if necessary to avoid crowding, add the beef and brown on all sides, about 2 minutes per side. Using a slotted spoon, transfer the meat to a plate and set aside.

Add the remaining 2 tablespoons oil to the pot and reduce the heat to medium. Add the onion and garlic and sauté until translucent, about 3 minutes. Add the carrots, celery, and parsnips and sauté, stirring occasionally to prevent burning, until the vegetables soften, 7 to 8 minutes. Add the thyme, bay leaf, and cloves, then return the meat and any accumulated juices on the plate to the pot and mix well. Add the salt and a few grinds of pepper and mix gently. Pour in the broth, raise the heat to high, and bring to a boil. Reduce the heat to low, cover partially, and simmer for 2 hours.

Add the barley, re-cover partially, and continue to simmer until the barley has expanded and is tender, about 45 minutes. Remove from the heat. Using a slotted spoon, remove and discard the thyme, bay leaf, and cloves. (Because they are very small, the cloves may require special attention to find and remove. Use a wooden spoon, if necessary.) Taste and adjust the seasoning with salt and pepper.

Ladle the soup into warmed bowls, garnish with the parsley, and serve right away.

SERVES 4

Beef and Barley Soup, page 70

WINE PROFILE

Cooper's Hawk Cabernet Sauvignon

This is a full-bodied wine redolent of black cherry, blackberry, blueberry, dried cranberry, anise, and vanilla. On the palate, flavors of dried cherry, black currant, tea leaves, and cinnamon are framed by fine-tuned acidity and smooth, ripe tannins. The finish is long and luxurious. Some of the wine's complexity comes from combining small amounts of Syrah, Barbera, Zinfandel, and Petit Verdot with the Cabernet, which makes up 75 percent of the blend. In winemaking, the sum of the parts is the key to the winemaker's art.

MEXICAN DRUNKEN SHRIMP WITH GUACAMOLE

This is one of our most popular signature dishes at Cooper's Hawk. The shrimp are "drunk" because we bathe them in a snappy tequila reduction. Creamy, crunchy guacamole heightens the flavors of the smoky bacon and shrimp, all dressed in a fine "drunken" sauce.

We typically serve this dish as an appetizer. It's a great way to start things off and pairs beautifully with all kinds of drinks, including cocktails and any of our select microbrews. Of course, wine is always an excellent option, too. Here, we've paired the dish with fruity Cooper's Hawk Gewürztraminer. The fragrant off-dry wine is loaded with spice and stands up nicely to the sweet, meaty shrimp and smoky bacon.

MEXICAN DRUNKEN
SHRIMP WITH GUACAMOLE

14 jumbo shrimp, heads removed, peeled, and deveined

7 slices bacon, halved crosswise

2 ripe avocados

3½ teaspoons fresh lime juice (1 to 2 limes)

½ cup plus 2 tablespoons diced tomato

2 tablespoons minced onion

4 teaspoons minced, seeded jalapeño chile

3 tablespoons minced fresh cilantro

¼ teaspoon salt

2 tablespoons canola oil

2 cloves garlic, minced

½ cup tequila

½ cup homemade or store-bought low-sodium chicken broth

3 tablespoons unsalted butter

Wrap each shrimp with a half slice of bacon. Place the wrapped shrimp on a tray, cover, and refrigerate.

To make the guacamole, cut the avocados in half and remove the pits. Using a teaspoon, scoop out the flesh into a medium nonreactive bowl. Using the back of a fork, mash the avocado and mix in 2½ teaspoons of the lime juice. Add ½ cup of the tomato, the onion, 2 teaspoons of the chile, 2 tablespoons of the cilantro, and the salt. Mix thoroughly, cover, and set aside.

In a large skillet, heat the canola oil over medium-high heat. When the oil is hot, add the bacon-wrapped shrimp and cook until they are browned and crisp on the bottom, about 3 minutes. Using tongs or a slotted spoon, turn the shrimp over and cook until crisp on the second side, another 2 minutes. Flip the shrimp back to the first side for another minute and then back to the second side for about 30 seconds. Using the tongs or spoon, transfer the shrimp to paper towels to drain.

Pour out the fat from the pan. Reduce the heat to medium, add the garlic, and sauté until the garlic starts to brown, about 15 seconds. Add the tequila, stir to dislodge any browned bits stuck to the pan bottom, and simmer until the tequila is reduced by half. Add the broth and reduce by half again. Add the butter and stir it as it melts into the liquid. Add the remaining 1 teaspoon lime juice, 2 teaspoons chile, and 2 tablespoons tomato. Stir occasionally to mix well and soften the tomato, about 1 minute. Remove from the heat.

On a large serving platter, set out 14 tablespoon-size dollops of guacamole. Top each guacamole dollop with a shrimp. Drizzle the tequila sauce over each shrimp and around the guacamole. Garnish each shrimp with a pinch of the remaining 1 tablespoon cilantro. Serve right away.

SERVES 4 TO 6 AS AN APPETIZER

WINE PROFILE

Cooper's Hawk Gewürztraminer

A classic blend of lychee nut and spice flavors awaits you with a glass of this lovely white wine. Gewürztraminer (not hard to pronounce if you read it slowly) is a grape that achieves its greatest expression in Germany and Alsace, France. The grapes used for this wine are grown in Northern California's Mendocino County, where cool weather can resemble the climate in northern Europe. Cooper's Hawk Gewürztraminer is made in an off-dry style—not too sweet and not too dry. It's fresh, clean, and perfect for all manner of fragrant seafood and poultry dishes, including the drunken shrimp featured here.

Karl Bruno
GENERAL MANAGER
KENWOOD INN, SONOMA VALLEY, CALIFORNIA

PORK BELLY SLIDERS WITH RED WINE BARBECUE SAUCE

These tasty little sliders are sure to please everyone. They come to us from our friend Karl Bruno, who manages the beautiful Kenwood Inn in Sonoma Valley, California. The valley lies at the heart of California's North Coast wine country, and this picturesque inn is nestled comfortably into its surroundings in proximity to the local vineyards.

Karl's pork belly sliders make the perfect appetizer but can also double as a main course accompanied by our soft, easy-drinking Cooper's Hawk Malbec. (If serving the sliders as a main course, try some of chef Kent Rathbun's coleslaw, page 115, on the side.) Crunchy, bright-edged cucumber plays a fine second fiddle to the smoky, salty pork belly all dressed up in a sweet, spicy, wine-touched barbecue sauce.

If your butcher does not carry pork belly (which is uncured bacon), he or she should be able to order it for you. You will need a quart of rendered duck fat, too, which can also be ordered or bought at specialty food stores.

This is not a difficult dish to prepare, but you'll need to allow for extended marination and chilling.

PORK BELLY SLIDERS WITH
RED WINE BARBECUE SAUCE

2 quarts water

½ cup kosher salt

1 cup sugar

8 green-tea tea bags

2 pounds pork belly, in a single piece

1 quart rendered duck fat

Red Wine Barbecue Sauce

½ cup dry red wine

½ cup hoisin sauce

½ cup favorite barbecue sauce

Cucumbers

½ cup rice vinegar

½ teaspoon fish sauce

¼ cup sugar

1 teaspoon salt

1 large cucumber, peeled and sliced
    into ¼-inch-thick rounds (at least 18
    slices)

18 potato or other small slider buns,
    warmed or at room temperature

In a large pot, combine the water, salt, and sugar, and bring to a boil, stirring to dissolve the salt and sugar. Remove from the heat, add the tea bags, and let steep for 1 hour.

Discard the tea bags and pour the liquid into a glass container large enough to hold the pork belly. Place the liquid in the refrigerator until cool. Add the pork belly to the cooled liquid, cover the container, and brine the pork belly in the refrigerator for at least 24 hours or up to 48 hours.

Preheat the oven to 275°F. Remove the pork belly from the brine and pat dry.

Place the pork belly in a Dutch oven or large ovenproof pan with high sides. Use a spoon or knife to coat the pork belly with the duck fat. Set the pan on the stove top over medium-high heat until the fat begins to melt and bubble. As soon as the fat is bubbling, remove the pan from the heat, cover, and transfer to the oven. Bake until the meat is very tender, about 4 hours. Remove the pan from the oven and let the pork belly cool to room temperature in the duck fat. Remove the pork belly from the pan (most of the fat will remain in the pan) and place it in a plastic container. Cover and refrigerate overnight. (You can discard the duck fat in the pan.)

To make the barbecue sauce, pour the wine into a medium saucepan, bring to a boil over medium-high heat, and boil until reduced by half, about 3 minutes. Add the hoisin sauce and barbecue sauce and stir well. Bring to a boil and simmer for 1 minute. Remove the pot from the heat and set aside.

About 15 minutes before serving time, prepare the cucumbers. In a medium nonreactive bowl, combine the vinegar, fish sauce, sugar, and salt and stir until the sugar and salt are dissolved. Add the cucumber slices and marinate for 10 to 15 minutes.

To assemble the dish, slice the pork belly into a minimum of eighteen 2-inch squares each ½ inch thick. Heat a large skillet over medium-high heat. Add the pork belly squares and cook, turning occasionally, until they are browned and somewhat crisp on both sides, about 2 minutes per side. Transfer the squares to a large platter.

Place a pork belly square on the bottom of each bun and top the meat with a cucumber slice and 1 teaspoon barbecue sauce. Close the slider with the top half of the bun. Serve right away.

MAKES 18 SLIDERS; SERVES 9 AS AN APPETIZER OR 4 OR 5 AS A MAIN COURSE

Jim and Jason Ebel
OWNERS
TWO BROTHERS BREWING COMPANY, WARRENVILLE, ILLINOIS

CHICKPEA AND SPINACH STEW

Chicago brewers-restaurateurs Jim and Jason Ebel produce our Cooper's Hawk Ale. Their Two Brothers Brewing Company and restaurants produce exquisitely crafted specialty beers and sensational American pub fare. After living in France in the mid-1990s, the brothers returned to the United States with a taste for international flavors.

This spicy, exotic bean "stew," which evokes the culinary excitement of a Middle Eastern marketplace, is an excellent side dish to accompany all manner of fish, poultry, or meat. To enjoy it as a main course, serve it with brown rice and a glass of our equally spicy Cooper's Hawk Zinfandel. And if you're not a fan of hot foods, just cut the paprika in half. Some heat will remain, but not the four-alarm kind. Purists might want to start with dried garbanzo beans (chickpeas), soaking them overnight before cooking. (If you cook your own, you need about 4 cups drained cooked beans and 1 cup of the cooking broth.) But canned beans make a perfectly respectable version—and are much more convenient!

CHICKPEA AND SPINACH STEW

1 pound spinach leaves

2 cans (15 ounces each) garbanzo
    beans (chickpeas)

2 cloves garlic, minced

1 tablespoon smoked hot paprika

1 tablespoon curry power

1 tablespoon ground cumin

2 tablespoons extra virgin olive oil

1 cup diced onion

1/2 cup tomato paste

1 cup water

1/2 cup red wine

1/2 teaspoon salt

1 tomato, coarsely chopped

4 cups cooked brown or white rice, if
    serving as a main course

Place the spinach leaves in a colander and rinse well under cold running water to remove any dirt or grit. Place the moist leaves in a large pot, cover, place over medium-high heat, and cook until wilted, about 2 minutes. Drain the spinach in the colander. When it is cool enough to hold, squeeze it with your hands to remove any additional liquid. Set aside.

Drain both cans of beans, reserving the liquid from 1 can (about 1 cup). Set the beans aside.

In a blender or food processor, combine the garlic, paprika, curry powder, cumin, and the reserved can liquid and process until smooth. Set aside.

In a large skillet, heat the olive oil over medium heat. Add the onion and sauté until translucent, about 3 minutes. Add the garbanzo beans and spinach and cook, stirring occasionally, for 1 minute. Add the tomato paste and mix thoroughly.

Add the puréed spice mixture, water, wine, and salt and mix thoroughly. Raise the heat to medium-high and bring the liquid to a gentle boil. Reduce the heat to medium and simmer for 15 minutes to blend the flavors.

Stir in the tomato and continue to simmer until any remaining liquid has reduced to a thick sauce, about 5 minutes. Serve hot accompanied with the rice, if desired.

SERVES 6 AS A SIDE DISH OR 4 AS A MAIN COURSE

Cooper's Hawk Zinfandel

Made from grapes grown in Amador County, where California's celebrated gold rush of 1849 began, this classy Zinfandel inherits the mantle of a tradition born some 150 years ago, when the first Zinfandel vines were planted in the region. Some of these old Zinfandel vines still bear fruit today. The wine is packed with mounds of cherry, plum, blackberry, spice, and toasty oak flavors. It's bright and zippy on the tongue and full of vibrant spices that highlight the fresh fruit.

RAVIOLI DI PICCOLO SOGNO

Chef Tony Priolo's popular Chicago restaurant is called Piccolo Sogno, or "Little Dream" in Italian. Here, he offers us a dreamy ravioli that transports us straight to Italy. Tony says, "You go to Italy for simple food, prepared by hand with local ingredients, and served with local wines."

In this case, Cooper's Hawk Cabernet Zinfandel puts a new twist on "local." Made at Cooper's Hawk Winery, it's about as local as any wine can get to Chicago, even though both grapes in the blend are grown in California. And in a nod to Italy, one of the grapes is Zinfandel, which is known to be genetically identical to the spicy Primitivo grapes grown in vineyards in Italy.

A hint of sweetness from the Marsala reduction highlights the fragrant cheeses used to fill the ravioli. Making pasta at home is fun, and this recipe is not hard to do. Timing is everything. You'll need at least an hour to prepare the dough—with or without a pasta machine. Semolina flour is used here. This coarse flour, made from durum wheat, is commonly used to make pasta and gives the dough its elasticity. It can be found in most major supermarkets. Make sure you roll out the dough as thinly as possible. Follow the steps in the order they are given for greatest ease in the kitchen.

Pasta Dough

2³/₄ cups semolina flour, plus more for
   kneading and rolling

1¹/₄ cups all-purpose flour

1 teaspoon sea salt

4 whole eggs

4 egg yolks, plus 1 yolk, lightly beaten,
   for brushing

1 tablespoon extra virgin olive oil

2 tablespoons water

Filling

1 cup fresh ricotta cheese

3 tablespoons grated Parmesan cheese

3 tablespoons fresh soft goat cheese
   (such as Laura Chenel's)

3 tablespoons chopped Gorgonzola
   Dolcelatte cheese

1 tablespoon minced fresh Italian
   parsley

Sea salt and freshly ground black
   pepper

Sauce

1 cup Marsala wine

¹/₂ cup homemade or store-bought low-
   sodium chicken broth

3 tablespoons unsalted butter

1 tablespoon pine nuts, toasted (see
   page 183)

Sea salt and freshly ground black
   pepper

Wedge of Parmesan cheese, preferably
   Parmigiano-Reggiano, finely shaved,
   for garnish

To make the dough, in a large bowl, using a fork, stir together thoroughly the semolina flour, all-purpose flour, and sea salt. Make a small well in the center of the dry ingredients and add the whole eggs, 4 egg yolks, olive oil, and water to the well. Using the fork, beat the liquid until smooth, then gradually draw the flour into the well, incorporating it with the egg mixture. Continue to draw the flour into the center until all of the flour is blended with the egg mixture and a moist but still crumbly dough forms.

Lightly flour a work surface with semolina flour. Remove the dough from the bowl and set it on the floured surface. Knead the dough with your hands, pushing it down with the heel of one hand, then pulling it together into a mound. Repeat until the dough is smooth and elastic, about 10 minutes. If the dough becomes too sticky, dust with additional semolina flour. When the dough is ready, let it sit at room temperature for 20 to 30 minutes.

While the dough rests, make the filling. In a medium bowl, combine the ricotta, Parmesan, goat, and Gorgonzola cheeses and mix together thoroughly with a fork. Mix in the parsley and season to taste with salt and pepper. Cover the bowl with plastic wrap and refrigerate until ready to use.

Ravioli di Piccolo Sogno, page 86

RAVIOLI DI PICCOLO SOGNO

To make the ravioli, divide the dough into 2 equal pieces, or into 4 equal pieces if your work surface is small or you are using a pasta machine. If using a pasta machine, secure it to the work surface according to the manufacturer's directions, adjust the rollers to the widest setting, and dust the rollers with semolina flour. Flatten a dough portion with your hand and pass the dough through the rollers. Fold the dough into thirds like a business letter, dust lightly with flour, and pass through the rollers again. Repeat a few more times until the dough is smooth, then reset the rollers one width narrower and pass the dough through the rollers. Continue feeding the dough through progressively narrower rollers until it is thin enough to see your hand through (usually the second-to-last setting). Lay the dough sheet on a floured work surface. Repeat with the remaining dough portions.

If you don't have a pasta machine, place a dough portion on a lightly floured work surface. Using a rolling pin, roll out the dough into a circular sheet that is thin enough to see your hand through. Lay the dough sheet on a floured surface. Repeat with the remaining dough portion(s).

Brush 1 dough sheet with some of the additional egg yolk. Using a teaspoon, arrange quarter-size dollops of the cheese filling on the sheet, spacing them 1½ to 2 inches apart. Lay a second sheet of dough over the filling-topped sheet. Using a small shot glass, gently press down over each mound of filling without breaking through the dough. This will eliminate air pockets. Then use a 2-inch round cookie cutter or inverted water glass to cut out round ravioli: press down firmly over each filling mound and then twist the cutter or glass to separate the ravioli from the surrounding dough. Place the ravioli on a floured baking sheet or parchment paper and set aside. Repeat until you run out of dough or filling.

To make the sauce and cook the ravioli, fill a 6-quart pot two-thirds full with lightly salted water and bring to a boil over high heat. Reduce the heat to low to keep the water hot while you prepare the sauce.

To make the sauce, in a small saucepan, bring the wine to a boil over high heat and boil until reduced by three-fourths, about 10 minutes. Remove from the heat and set aside. In another small saucepan, bring the broth to a boil over high heat and boil until reduced by half, about 5 minutes. Remove from the heat and set aside.

Bring the water in the pot back to a boil and add the ravioli. Depending on the thickness of your dough, the ravioli will require 2 to 5 minutes to soften and float to the surface. Prior to removing all of the ravioli from the water, scoop one out and taste it to make sure the dough is al dente and the filling is piping hot. Then, using a slotted spoon, lift the ravioli out of the pot and gently lay them in a colander to drain. (Do not rinse.)

To finish the sauce, return the broth to medium-high heat. Add the butter and stir gently with a wooden spoon or whisk as it melts. Stir in the nuts and remove from the heat. Season to taste with salt and pepper.

To serve, arrange 6 or 7 ravioli in a circle on each warmed individual plate, overlapping on one side only. Drizzle the butter sauce and pine nuts over each serving. Reheat the Marsala glaze over high heat for 10 seconds and spoon an equal portion over each serving. Garnish with the Parmesan shavings and serve at once.

MAKES ABOUT 30 RAVIOLI; SERVES 4 OR 5

WINE PROFILE

Cooper's Hawk Cabernet Zinfandel

This unusual blend of grapes serves up a uniquely styled, highly satisfying glass of wine. Firm Cabernet gives it structure, while the Zinfandel (also known as Primitivo in its native Italy) offers a lovely fruity component. The wine shows off a bit of that classic "jammy" Zinfandel style tempered by Cabernet's signature herbal notes. The Zinfandel grapes come from Amador County in California's Sierra foothills (where gold was discovered in 1849). The Cabernet hails from one of grower Andy Beckstoffer's celebrated Napa Valley vineyards.

José Esparza
CULINARY AREA DIRECTOR
COOPER'S HAWK WINERY & RESTAURANTS

LINGUINE AI FRUTTI DI MARE

Chef José Esparza's career began over twenty years ago as a dishwasher for the Fairmont Hotel in Chicago. He soon discovered a passion and talent for cooking and moved up the ranks at such renowned kitchens as the Hyatt, Carlucci's, Wildfire and Aramark, where he first met Tim. He later joined Cooper's Hawk, where the two are delighted to work together again. When he's not cooking, mentoring younger chefs, or spending time with his family, José can be found pursuing his favorite hobby: jogging.

José's creamy-rich pasta is brimming with the flavors of the sea. Meaty shrimp, tender day boat scallops, and crabmeat are paired with artichoke hearts and asparagus to create a thoroughly satisfying treat for the senses. The dish is topped with a colorful array of red peppers, tomatoes, and parsley—all artfully matched with our fresh, light-bodied Cooper's Hawk White.

Large, tender day boat sea scallops, which are harvested by small boats that leave and return to port the same day to guarantee the freshest catch, are ideal for this dish. You can, however, use 10 ounces of smaller bay scallops in their place.

LINGUINE AI FRUTTI DI MARE

8 ounces asparagus, tough bottoms
    trimmed and cut into 1-inch lengths

1 pound dried linguine

2 tablespoons extra virgin olive oil

2 cloves garlic, minced

8 day boat sea scallops (about 10
    ounces), quartered

12 large shrimp, heads removed,
    peeled, and deveined

½ cup white wine

1 tablespoon unsalted butter

¾ cup homemade or store-bought low-
    sodium chicken broth

1¼ cups heavy cream

¼ cup grated Asiago cheese

¼ cup grated Parmesan cheese

¼ teaspoon salt

8 well-drained water-packed canned
    artichoke hearts, halved lengthwise

1 roasted red pepper, homemade
    (page 184) or store-bought, diced
    (about ¾ cup)

4 ounces fresh-cooked lump crabmeat,
    picked over for shell fragments and
    cartilage (about 1 cup)

12 cherry tomatoes, halved

2 tablespoons minced fresh Italian
    parsley

Freshly ground black pepper

Fill a small saucepan half full with water and bring to a boil over high heat. Add the asparagus and cook until tender, about 2 minutes. Drain in a colander and rinse under cold running water until cool. Set aside.

Fill a large pot with lightly salted water and bring to a boil over high. Add the pasta and cook until al dente, about 10 minutes or according to package directions.

While the water for the pasta is heating, begin preparing the sauce. In a large skillet, heat the olive oil over medium-high heat. Add the garlic and sauté until fragrant, about 30 seconds. Add the scallops and shrimp and cook, stirring regularly, until the shrimp turn pink and the scallops turn opaque, about 3 minutes. Using a slotted spoon, transfer the shrimp and scallops to a bowl and keep warm.

Add the wine to the pan and simmer over medium-high heat until reduced by half, about 3 minutes. Stir in the butter until it melts.

Add the broth, cream, Asiago and Parmesan cheeses, and salt and mix well. Bring to a gentle boil, reduce the heat to medium-low, and cook, stirring occasionally, until the sauce begins to thicken, about 5 minutes. Add the asparagus and artichokes to the sauce and simmer, stirring occasionally, until heated through, about 5 minutes longer.

When the pasta is ready, drain in a colander (do not rinse with water) and transfer to a large serving bowl. Add the sauce and toss with the pasta to mix thoroughly. Add the roasted pepper and the shrimp and scallops and any accumulated juices and mix well. Sprinkle with the crabmeat and garnish with the tomatoes, parsley, and a few grinds of pepper. Serve immediately.

SERVES 4 TO 6

Cooper's Hawk White

Fresh, clean, and light bodied, this versatile white wine pairs well with many lighter-styled foods, such as chef José Esparza's seafood pasta. It also makes a wonderful aperitif. Look for bright citrus and mineral notes here, backed by subtle hints of apple and herb. We combine several varietals to make this adaptable wine. Each vintage yields a new blend yet maintains stylistic continuity year in and year out.

PASTA FRITTATA

Have an omelet with your spaghetti. Or better yet, have both in one! This versatile recipe comes to us from Breakfast Queen Ina Pinkney, chef-owner of Ina's in Chicago. In 1991, Ina opened Ina's Kitchen, which quickly became Chicago's premier breakfast restaurant. She even appeared in a national Quaker Oats commercial as herself, the Breakfast Queen. Today, Ina's is an American food restaurant serving breakfast, lunch, and occasional dinners in Chicago's trendy West Loop Market District.

Ina's Pasta Frittata is the perfect brunch or lunch. But it can also be an excellent dinner choice, especially when paired with a glass of fruit-forward Cooper's Hawk Merlot.

The pasta gives this oven-baked omelet a certain fullness. Three different cheeses make it delightfully creamy, and a colorful selection of vegetables gives it allure. The tomato sauce is on the bottom, just to keep things interesting! Make the tomato sauce before you make the frittata, then reheat the sauce on the stove top just before serving.

PASTA FRITTATA

Tomato Sauce

2 tablespoons extra virgin olive oil

½ onion, diced

3 cloves garlic, minced

1 can (28 ounces) whole tomatoes, drained

1 teaspoon dried oregano

½ teaspoon salt

½ teaspoon freshly ground black pepper

Frittata

8 ounces dried spaghetti

3 tablespoons extra virgin olive oil

¾ cup chopped onion

2 cloves garlic, minced

½ cup thinly sliced red pepper

1½ cups sliced mushrooms

1½ cups thinly sliced zucchini rounds

1 teaspoon dried oregano

10 eggs

¾ cup whole milk

1 teaspoon salt

½ teaspoon freshly ground black pepper

1½ cups grated Cheddar cheese (about 6 ounces)

½ cup grated Parmesan cheese

4 ounces cream cheese, cut into ½-inch cubes

Grated Parmesan cheese for garnish

To make the sauce, in a large skillet, heat the olive oil over medium heat. Add the onion and garlic and sauté until the onion is translucent, 2 to 3 minutes. Stir in the tomatoes, oregano, salt, and pepper. Using a fork or potato masher, gently mash the tomatoes. (Go easy or you might send tomato juice all over the kitchen.) Reduce the heat to medium-low and simmer, uncovered, until thick, about 10 minutes. Set aside until ready to serve.

To make the frittata, fill a large pot with lightly salted water and bring to a boil over high. Add the pasta and cook until al dente, about 10 minutes or according to package directions. Drain in a colander and set aside.

Preheat the oven to 350°F. Lightly brush a 10-inch round baking pan with 1 tablespoon of the olive oil.

In a skillet, heat the remaining 2 tablespoons olive oil over medium heat. Add the onion and garlic and sauté until translucent, 2 to 3 minutes. Add the red pepper, mushrooms, and zucchini and sauté, stirring occasionally, until soft, about 10 minutes. Add the oregano and mix thoroughly. Remove from the heat and set aside.

In a large bowl, using a whisk or electric mixer, beat together the eggs, milk, salt, pepper, Cheddar, and Parmesan until all the ingredients are incorporated. Using a wooden spoon, stir in the cream cheese.

Lay the spaghetti on the bottom of the prepared baking pan. Spoon the cooked vegetables on top of the noodles. Stir the egg-cheese mixture one more time to keep the cream cheese evenly distributed, then pour the mixture over the vegetables and noodles.

Using your hands, gently pat down the egg-cheese mixture to cover the vegetables and noodles as well as you can. Bake the frittata until it is firm to the touch and lightly brown on top, 30 to 40 minutes. Remove the pan from the oven and let cool for a few minutes. Meanwhile, reheat the tomato sauce until hot.

Cut the frittata into 4 to 6 wedges. Spread the reheated tomato sauce in a circle over the bottom of each dinner plate. Place a frittata wedge on top of the sauce and garnish with additional Parmesan cheese.

SERVES 4 TO 6

WINE PROFILE

Cooper's Hawk Merlot

Merlot forms the backbone of Bordeaux's right bank wineries, which blend it with smaller amounts of Cabernet Sauvignon and other related grapes. On its own, it offers a pure expression of ripe cherry flavors subtly nuanced with other fruits and toasty oak. Cooper's Hawk Merlot starts off with wonderful cherry aromas that are followed by a tightly wound array of blackberry, plum, and black cherry flavors on the palate. A hint of smoky oak rounds it off nicely, delivering a smooth finish.

PIZZA AGLIARULO

Colorfully anointed with the red, white, and green of the Italian flag, this pizza is shared with us by Jonathan Goldsmith, owner of Spacca Napoli Pizzeria in Chicago. The restaurant has a *MICHELIN Guide* Bib Gourmand rating and was originally inspired by Jonathan's long-standing love of Italy, where he spends as much time as possible. Not surprisingly, we have paired this pizza with an Italian wine varietal. Sangiovese has just the right mix of bright fruit and acidity to tandem seamlessly with Jonathan's pizza.

Agliarulo is the family name of the third- and fourth-generation artisans from Naples who came to Chicago to build the oven at Spacca Napoli. They consider this pizza to be among their favorites, and Jonathan has selected it to honor the Agliarulo family. Jonathan's own family also plays an important role in this book, with recipes by his aunt, Joyce Goldstein (page 163), and his cousin, Evan Goldstein (page 159).

It's the crust that makes this pie special. Jonathan uses white, silky Italian "00" flour, which is available in many supermarkets. It yields a particularly soft, supple crust with just enough chew at the edges.

PIZZA AGLIARULO

Dough

1 teaspoon fast-acting (instant) dry
  yeast

1⅓ cups plus ¼ cup water, at room
  temperature (about 70°F)

3 cups (about 1 pound) Italian "00"
  flour, plus more for kneading and
  shaping

1 tablespoon fine sea salt

Topping

1 tablespoon extra virgin olive oil

1 pound medium shrimp, heads
  removed, peeled, and deveined

½ cup heavy cream

4 ounces mascarpone cheese (about
  ½ cup)

1 pint (about 2 cups) cherry tomatoes,
  halved

8 ounces mozzarella cheese, cut into
  ½-inch cubes

1 cup arugula

To make the dough, in a large bowl, combine the yeast with 1⅓ cups of the water. Let sit for about 10 minutes to allow the yeast to become active. (You will see the beginnings of small bubbles.) Using a wooden spoon, slowly stir in the flour, adding the salt when you've used about half of the flour. Continue to stir until a sticky dough begins to form. When the dough becomes too thick and dry to stir with the spoon, add the remaining ¼ cup water and, using your hands, shape the dough into a large ball in the bowl.

Lightly flour a work surface with flour (and do the same to your hands if they have become too sticky). Remove the dough from the bowl and set it on the floured surface. Knead the dough with your hands, pushing it down with the heel of one hand, then pulling it together into a mound. Repeat until the dough is firm yet elastic and small air bubbles are visible when the dough is cut open, 10 to 15 minutes. Transfer the dough to a clean, large bowl and cover with a damp cloth. Set aside in a cool, draft-free area (but at room temperature). After 1 hour, cut the dough in half and shape each half into a ball. Place each ball in a large bowl (it needs room to rise) and cover the bowls with plastic wrap. Let rise at room temperature for 8 hours.

When you are ready to bake the pizzas, preheat the oven to 500°F.

To make the topping, in a skillet, heat the olive oil over medium–high heat. Add the shrimp and cook, turning once, just until they begin to turn pink, 30 to 60 seconds on each side. (Don't overcook them because they will continue to cook in the oven.) Transfer the shrimp to a bowl and set aside.

To make the creamy light pizza sauce, *panna cucina*, in a bowl, whisk together the cream and mascarpone cheese until smooth. Set aside.

Lightly dust a work surface with flour. Place a dough ball on the floured surface and, using your fingertips, flatten and shape the ball into a flat crust. Push out from the center of the dough to extend it into a larger circle, stretching and flattening as you go. Flip the dough occasionally to keep it from becoming sticky. An easier method is to use a rolling pin, which produces a result closer to the thinner, crispier crust of Roman pizza. When the crust is about 15 inches in diameter and quite thin, crimp the rim with your thumb and forefinger to create a slightly raised edge. This will prevent the sauce from running off the crust. Repeat with the remaining dough ball. Transfer the pie crusts to two nonstick, 16-inch pizza pans. (If using 1 or 2 pizza stones, you will not use pizza pans. But the stone(s) will need to be preheated in the oven, and the pizzas will need to be fully prepared before sliding them onto the stone(s).

Divide the sauce evenly between the crusts and spread it lightly over the surface. Divide the shrimp evenly between the crusts. Do the same with the tomatoes and then the mozzarella cheese. Place the pizzas in the oven and cook until the edges of the crusts and the tops of the pies start to show some browning, 12 to 15 minutes.

Remove the pizzas from the oven and scatter the arugula over the top, dividing it evenly. Cut into wedges and serve at once.

MAKES TWO 14-INCH PIZZAS; SERVES 4 AS A MAIN COURSE OR 8 AS AN APPETIZER

WINE PROFILE

Cooper's Hawk Sangiovese

Sangiovese is the signature grape of Tuscany. In the United States, it has found a home in many states, where it produces wines of distinction. Our Cooper's Hawk Sangiovese is made from grapes grown in Washington and California. The wine kicks off with bright cherry and herb notes, then fans out along the palate to reveal pretty toast, more red fruit, and spice flavors. Firm tannins frame the ensemble to create excellent structure.

Rob Warren
WINEMAKER
COOPER'S HAWK WINERY & RESTAURANTS

THREE-CHEESE PIZZA WITH ROASTED RED PEPPERS, PROSCIUTTO, AND CANDIED WALNUTS

This original pizza pairs perfectly with the rustic character of our Cooper's Hawk Winemaker's Barrel Reserve red wine. At every Cooper's Hawk restaurant, diners can enjoy this unique wine drawn directly from the barrel in which it is aged. And it's no accident that this recipe was contributed by Cooper's Hawk winemaker Rob Warren, who takes a special interest in what he eats and drinks!

Three cheeses offer a rich diversity of flavors here, and the salty, earthy prosciutto makes a great topping. So do the candied walnuts, which you can make at home or purchase ready-made. Remember to prepare them in advance if you are making them from scratch.

Rob says, "The walnuts provide a little bitterness to help reduce the perceived bitterness on the wine's finish. The texture, flavors, and sweetness of the nuts bring out the earthiness in the wine and help accentuate those characteristics in the Fontina."

THREE-CHEESE PIZZA WITH ROASTED RED PEPPERS, PROSCIUTTO, AND CANDIED WALNUTS

Dough

¹/₂ envelope (1¹/₄ teaspoons) active dry
    yeast

³/₄ cup warm water

¹/₄ cup high-gluten flour

1 cup all-purpose flour, plus more for
    kneading and rolling

1 tablespoon extra virgin olive oil, plus
    more for the bowl and pan

¹/₄ teaspoon salt

To make the dough, in a large bowl, combine the yeast with ½ cup of the warm water. Let sit until you see bubbles rising, about 5 minutes. Using a wooden spoon, stir in the high-gluten flour. Add the all-purpose flour, the 1 tablespoon olive oil, and the salt. Stir until a sticky dough begins to form. Add the remaining ¼ cup warm water and, using your hands, shape the dough into a ball.

When your hands become too sticky, dust them with flour and continue to knead, pushing the dough down with the heel of your hand, then pulling it together into a mound. Repeat until the dough is firm yet elastic, 3 to 4 minutes.

Lightly oil another large bowl. Place the dough in the bowl, cover with plastic wrap, and set it in a reasonably warm room to rise until doubled in size, about 2 hours.

Preheat the oven to 500°F.

Lightly flour a work surface with flour. Turn the risen dough out onto the floured surface, shape it again into a ball, and then flatten it into a thick disk. Using a rolling pin, roll out the dough into a thin round about 15 inches in diameter. Crimp the rim with your thumb and forefinger to create a slightly raised edge. Transfer the crust to a 16-inch nonstick pizza pan.

Topping

1 clove garlic, minced

1 teaspoon crushed red pepper flakes

¼ cup extra virgin olive oil

¾ cup shredded mozzarella cheese
(about 6 ounces)

½ cup shredded Italian Fontina cheese
(about 4 ounces)

1 cup roasted red peppers, homemade
(page 184) or store-bought, cut
lengthwise into ¼-inch-wide strips

4 ounces Italian prosciutto, cut into
narrow strips

½ cup chopped fresh basil

¼ cup candied walnuts, homemade
(page 187) or store-bought, coarsely
chopped

½ cup crumbled soft fresh goat cheese
(about 4 ounces)

To make the topping, in a small bowl, stir the garlic and red pepper flakes into the olive oil. Brush the olive oil mixture over the prepared pizza crust. In a medium bowl, use your hands to mix together the mozzarella and Fontina cheeses. Sprinkle three-fourths of the cheese mix evenly over the pizza crust. Evenly distribute the red pepper strips over the cheese. Then do the same with the prosciutto and basil. Sprinkle the remaining cheese mix over the basil. Top evenly with the walnuts and the goat cheese.

Bake in the oven until the edges of the crust are golden brown, about 12 minutes. Remove from the oven, cut into wedges, and serve at once.

MAKES ONE 14-INCH PIZZA; SERVES 2 AS A MAIN COURSE OR 4 AS AN APPETIZER

CRAB CAKES WITH LEMON BUTTER AND MANGO SALSA

These scrumptious crab cakes are contributed by a pair of Lynfred Winery stars: winemaker Andrés Basso and chef Christopher Smith. I was fortunate to learn my early winemaking skills at Lynfred, where I worked in tandem with Andrés.

A native of Chile who has also made wine in the Napa Valley, Washington, and Virginia, Andrés has a unique breadth of experience that he generously shared with me when Cooper's Hawk was still more of a dream than a reality. He ensured that I acquired the tools that I needed to set up the original Cooper's Hawk Winery, and we are all grateful to him for his help.

Seated in a richly textured lemon butter sauce, these scrumptious crab cakes are topped with a tangy mango salsa that gives the dish a special lift. The flavors are highlighted by the bright, fresh citrus and herb notes in the wine. Use the biggest pan you have (at least fifteen inches in diameter if possible) for cooking the crab cakes, as it is hard to flip them when they are crowded together. If you don't have a really big pan, use two pans.

Andrés Basso

CRAB CAKES WITH LEMON
BUTTER AND MANGO SALSA

Mango Salsa

2 cups diced mango

½ cup diced onion

¼ cup minced fresh cilantro

2 tablespoons fresh lime juice

1 clove garlic, finely minced

Salt and freshly ground black pepper

Crab Cakes

2 tablespoons extra virgin olive oil

½ cup diced onion

3 cloves garlic, minced

½ cup chopped red pepper

½ cup chopped green pepper

1 teaspoon Worcestershire sauce

Pinch of cayenne pepper

1 cup *panko* (Japanese bread crumbs)

1½ pounds fresh-cooked lump
   crabmeat, picked over for shell frag-
   ments and cartilage

½ cup chopped green onions, white
   and tender green parts only

¼ teaspoon salt

Freshly ground black pepper

2 eggs, lightly beaten

To make the salsa, in a bowl, combine the mango, onion, cilantro, lime juice, and garlic and mix well. Season to taste with salt and pepper. Cover and refrigerate for up to 6 hours.

To make the crab cakes, line a baking sheet with parchment paper. In a large skillet, heat the olive oil over medium-high heat. Add the onion, garlic, and red and green peppers and sauté until the peppers are tender, 3 to 4 minutes. Reduce the heat to medium, add the Worcestershire sauce, cayenne pepper, and *panko*, mix well, and sauté for 2 minutes. Remove from the heat.

Add the crabmeat, green onions, and the salt to the pan and mix thoroughly, then season with ground pepper. Stir the eggs into the crab mixture, mixing well. Using a ⅓-cup measuring cup as a mold, scoop up and shape the crab mixture into about fifteen ¾-inch-thick crab cakes. As the cakes are shaped, place them on the prepared baking sheet. Cover the baking sheet with plastic wrap and chill for at least 2 hours or up to 1 day before continuing.

To make the lemon butter, in a medium skillet, combine the wine, lemon juice, shallot, and bay leaf, bring the liquid to a boil over medium-high heat, and boil until reduced by half, about 3 minutes. Remove and discard the bay leaf. Reduce the heat to medium-low and add the butter, a few pieces at a time, whisking after each addition until completely melted. (Do not allow the butter to boil.) Whisk in the cream, then remove the pan from the heat and set aside. The sauce can be made up to 2 hours in advance and left at room temperature until ready to serve.

To cook the crab cakes, in a very large skillet, heat the olive oil over high heat until it begins to shimmer. Place the crab cakes in the pan and lower the heat to medium-high. Using a spatula, gently press down on top of each cake to flatten it slightly and firm it up. Cook until the bottoms are golden, 7 to 8 minutes. Carefully flip the cakes over and cook on the second side until golden, 4 to 5 minutes.

Lemon Butter

¼ cup dry white wine

¼ cup fresh lemon juice

2 tablespoons minced shallot

1 bay leaf

1 cup (2 sticks) chilled unsalted butter, cut into small pieces

2 tablespoons heavy cream

¼ cup extra virgin olive oil

While the crab cakes are cooking, remove the mango salsa from the refrigerator. Warm the lemon butter over medium-low heat, whisking regularly to prevent boiling.

To serve, spoon 3 to 4 tablespoons of the lemon butter onto each warmed dinner plate. Divide the crab cakes evenly among the plates, placing them on top of the lemon butter. Garnish each cake with a spoonful of salsa. Serve right away.

SERVES 4 TO 6

WINE PROFILE

Cooper's Hawk Pinot Gris

Pinot Gris means "gray grape" in French, and in Italian it is Pinot Grigio. Regardless of what you call it, the grape is not gray, although it can take on a slightly pink hue when ripe. But the resulting wine is white. Cooper's Hawk Pinot Gris is made from grapes grown on California's Central Coast. The wine is bright and fresh, with hints of citrus and herb flavors highlighted by a steely, flinty center, and a clean and quite refreshing finish.

Kent Rathbun
CHEF AND OWNER
JASPER'S, DALLAS, TEXAS

FRIED CATFISH WITH LEMON-JALAPEÑO COLESLAW AND RED PEPPER TARTAR SAUCE

Kent Rathbun is well known for his illustrious Texas restaurants that include Abacus, Jasper's, Rathbun's Blue Plate Kitchen, and KB's Woodfire Grill. He and his brother, Kevin, are also famous for having competed on the Food Network's hit series *Iron Chef America* and defeating Bobby Flay in a frenetic culinary battle. As a guest chef at Cooper's Hawk, Kent has created memorable meals inside the actual winery itself. This recipe is inspired by his youth, growing up in Kansas City, Missouri.

"When I was a kid, the first fish I ever caught was catfish," the chef recalls. "I can't tell you how many catfish fries we had at my grandma's. This is country cooking, the way my brother and I grew up."

Despite the long list of ingredients here, this recipe is easy to make. Two ingredients warrant clarification: Cajun seasoning is nothing more than cayenne pepper blended with a little salt and sugar. Creole mustard is a grainy mustard. Kent's favorite brand is Zatarain's, but any coarse-grained mustard will do.

Enjoy this dish with fruity Cooper's Hawk Viognier, which provides a fine backdrop for chef Rathbun's upfront flavors.

FRIED CATFISH WITH LEMON-JALAPEÑO COLESLAW AND RED PEPPER TARTAR SAUCE

Roasted Red Pepper Tartar Sauce

2 roasted red peppers, homemade (page 184) or store-bought

1 cup mayonnaise, homemade (page 183) or store-bought

1 tablespoon fresh lemon juice

2 tablespoons minced fresh Italian parsley

1 tablespoon minced capers

1/2 teaspoon Worcestershire sauce

1/4 teaspoon Tabasco sauce

1/4 cup finely chopped red onion

2 teaspoons Cajun seasoning

Salt

Fish

1 1/2 cups dry white wine

3/4 cup coarse-grained mustard

8 skinned catfish fillets (about 2 pounds)

1 cup coarse-grind yellow cornmeal

1/2 cup cornstarch

2 tablespoons Cajun seasoning

Canola oil for frying

To make the tartar sauce, in a blender or food processor, purée the red peppers. In a bowl, combine the purée, mayonnaise, lemon juice, parsley, capers, Worcestershire sauce, Tabasco sauce, onion, and Cajun seasoning and mix well. Season to taste with salt. Cover and refrigerate until ready to serve.

To marinate the fish, in a large nonreactive bowl, whisk together the wine and mustard. Place the fillets in the marinade, cover, and refrigerate for about 1 hour.

To make the cornmeal dredging mix, in wide, shallow bowl, stir together the cornmeal, cornstarch, and Cajun seasoning with a fork. Set aside until you are ready to cook the fish.

While the fish is marinating, prepare the coleslaw. In a small bowl, stir together the lemon juice, sour cream, and mayonnaise. Add the sugar, vinegar, chile, salt, white pepper, and lemon zest and stir to mix well. Set aside.

In a large bowl, combine the cabbage, carrot, apple, and cilantro. Add the sour cream–mayonnaise dressing and toss gently to mix thoroughly. Cover and refrigerate until ready to serve.

To fry the fish, preheat the oven to 175°F. Line a heatproof platter or a baking sheet with paper towels. Pour the canola oil to a depth of about 1 1/2

WINE PROFILE

Cooper's Hawk Viognier

Viognier is a white grape that was once found only in a tiny region of the Rhône Valley in France. In the last few decades, it has found its way to the New World and now thrives in California.

Cooper's Hawk Viognier is made from grapes grown in two California wine regions: coastal Santa Barbara and—farther north and inland—Clarksburg. This pretty, round-textured wine is blessed with lovely peach, nectarine, and spice flavors. It is medium bodied, elegant on the palate, and long on the finish.

Coleslaw

1 tablespoon fresh lemon juice

¾ cup sour cream

½ cup mayonnaise, homemade (page 183) or store-bought

1 teaspoon sugar

2 teaspoons white wine vinegar

1 jalapeño chile, seeded and minced (about 2 tablespoons)

½ teaspoon salt

½ teaspoon ground white pepper

1 tablespoon chopped lemon zest

1 small head green cabbage (about 2 pounds), cut into narrow strips

1 carrot, peeled and grated

1 large Granny Smith apple, peeled, halved, cored, and grated

⅓ cup chopped fresh cilantro

inches into a large, deep, heavy skillet and heat over medium-high heat until it starts to shimmer. Carefully remove a fish fillet from the marinade and gently dredge it in the cornmeal mix until it is evenly coated on both sides. Place the fillet in the hot oil. Repeat with more fillets, being careful not to crowd the pan. Fry the fillets until they are light brown on the first side, 2 to 3 minutes. Using tongs or a spatula, turn and fry the fillets until brown and crisp on the second side. Watch the fillets closely. The second side will cook more quickly than the first side—no more than 2 minutes.

Using the tongs or spatula, transfer the fillets to the towel-lined serving platter to drain, then keep warm in the oven. Let the oil return to shimmering hot before frying the remaining fillets the same way.

Place a single serving of coleslaw on each plate with 1 or 2 fish fillets next to it. Drizzle the tartar sauce over the fillets and serve right away.

SERVES 4 TO 6

Bill and Becky Courtright
OWNERS

Jerome Bacle
EXECUTIVE CHEF

COURTRIGHT'S, WILLOW SPRINGS, ILLINOIS

In winter, the markets of southern France are filled with salt cod for making *brandade*, a purée that is generally eaten with potatoes or bread. This recipe is shared with us by our friends Bill and Becky Courtright and executive chef Jerome Bacle of Courtright's restaurant, in Willow Springs, Illinois. Founded in 1995, Courtright's was recently awarded its first Michelin star. In addition to providing its customers with the ultimate in American fine dining, Bill and Becky have created a restaurant where an egalitarian philosophy gives everyone who works there a sense of responsibility that is reflected in a consummate dining experience.

In this recipe, the salt-cured cod shares top honors with fresh halibut. Look for salt cod in your local specialty food shops or any fine supermarket. The fish is dressed up with chorizo, a deliciously earthy, spicy pork sausage also found in most supermarkets.

In addition to providing their customers with excellent meals, the Courtrights are renowned for their extensive collection of fine wines. We've paired this recipe with our exceptional Cooper's Hawk Lux Chardonnay. The well-structured, lush-textured wine offers an excellent match for a dish brimming with good taste.

ROASTED HALIBUT WITH SAFFRON BRANDADE, CARAMELIZED PEARL ONIONS, AND CHORIZO EMULSION

8 ounces salt cod fillet

2 large russet potatoes

1 cup pearl onions

5 tablespoons extra virgin olive oil

¼ cup minced shallots

½ cup minced red onion

2 cloves garlic, minced

1 bay leaf

¾ teaspoon dried thyme

⅛ teaspoon cayenne pepper

½ red pepper, seeded and finely chopped

1 cup diced chorizo

¾ cup dry white wine

2 cups homemade or store-bought low-sodium chicken broth

3 tablespoons unsalted butter

1½ cups whole milk

Pinch of saffron threads

2 egg yolks

2 tablespoons unsalted butter, at room temperature

2 tablespoons minced fresh Italian parsley

4 halibut fillets, 5 to 6 ounces each

Salt and freshly ground black pepper

Place the salt cod in a plastic container or glass bowl and add cold water to cover by 2 inches. Cover the container and refrigerate overnight.

Preheat the oven to 400°F.

Rinse the potatoes but do not peel. Poke holes in the sides of each potato with a fork, then wrap individually in aluminum foil. Bake until the potatoes are soft to the touch, about 1½ hours.

While the potatoes are baking, prepare the pearl onions and chorizo emulsion. (But you will need to wait until the potatoes are done to make the *brandade*.) To prepare the onions, cut a small, shallow X in the root end of each onion. In a small to medium saucepan, bring 2 cups water to a boil. Drop the onions into the water and cook for 1 minute, then drain and rinse under cold running water. Gently squeeze the onions from their skins. If necessary, use a small paring knife to remove the root. Set the onions aside.

To make the chorizo emulsion, in a medium skillet, heat 2 tablespoons of the olive oil over medium heat. Add the shallots and red onion and sauté until wilted, about 3 minutes. Add half of the garlic and stir until fragrant, about 30 seconds. Add the bay leaf, thyme, and cayenne and mix well. Add the red pepper and chorizo and mix until all of the ingredients are coated with herbs. Add ½ cup of the wine and bring to a boil. Simmer until the wine has reduced by half, about 2 minutes. Add the broth, bring to a boil, reduce the heat to a steady simmer, and cook uncovered, stirring occasionally, for 20 minutes. Add the butter and simmer for 5 minutes

Roasted Halibut with Saffron
Brandade, Caramelized Pearl
Onions, and Chorizo Emulsion,
page 117

ROASTED HALIBUT WITH SAFFRON BRANDADE, CARAMELIZED PEARL ONIONS, AND CHORIZO EMULSION

longer. The sauce should be thick but still have some liquid. Remove from the heat and let cool slightly.

Transfer the chorizo mixture to a blender or food processor and purée until smooth. Strain the purée through a fine-mesh sieve, return the strained liquid to the pan, and discard the solids remaining in the sieve. Set the sauce aside.

To make the *brandade*, remove the salt cod from the water and cut it into ¼-inch cubes, removing any errant bones and skin. Pour the milk into a medium saucepan, add the cod, and bring to a simmer over medium heat. Simmer until the fish flakes when nudged with a fork, about 10 minutes. Remove from the heat and reserve.

While the fish is simmering, in a small saucepan, combine the remaining ¼ cup wine and the saffron, bring to a boil over medium-high heat, and boil until the wine has reduced by half, about 5 minutes. Remove from the heat and set aside.

At this point, the potatoes should be out of the oven, unwrapped, and cool enough to handle. Leave the oven set at 400°F for cooking the halibut. Cut each potato in half lengthwise and spoon the white flesh into a large nonreactive bowl. Discard the skins. Using a slotted spoon, remove the salt cod from the milk, reserving the warm milk. Using a wooden spoon, stir the salt cod and saffron-wine mixture into the potatoes. Add the egg yolks, butter, and 1 tablespoon of the parsley and mix well. Add 6 tablespoons of the

warm milk to the potato mixture and stir until the mixture is fairly smooth. Cover to keep warm and set aside. Discard the remaining milk.

Season the halibut fillets on both sides with salt and pepper. In a large ovenproof skillet, heat 2 tablespoons of the olive oil over medium-high heat. When the oil starts to shimmer, place the fillets in the hot pan and sear on the first side for 1 minute. Flip the fillets and sear the second side for 30 seconds. Transfer the pan to the oven and bake until the fish is just opaque throughout when tested with a knife tip, about 8 minutes.

While the halibut is baking, in a small skillet, heat the remaining 1 tablespoon olive oil over medium heat. Add the remaining garlic and the remaining 1 tablespoon parsley and sauté for 30 seconds. Add the pearl onions and mix well to coat the onions evenly with the oil and parsley. Simmer over medium-low heat just until heated through and tender, about 3 minutes.

To serve, reheat the chorizo emulsion over low heat. The *brandade* should still be warm, but if necessary, reheat it over medium-low heat. Place about ⅔ cup *brandade* on each warmed individual plate and flatten it slightly to create a patty about 1 inch thick and 5 to 6 inches in diameter. Top with the pearl onions, dividing them evenly, then lay a halibut fillet on top of the onions. Drizzle each fillet with 2 tablespoons of the chorizo emulsion. You can also drizzle the emulsion in a circle around the *brandade* patty. Serve right away.

SERVES 4

WINE PROFILE

Cooper's Hawk Lux Chardonnay

Chardonnay is arguably the world's best-known white grape. And most famous among the world's Chardonnays are those made in Burgundy. But New World Chardonnays have established themselves among the wine elite, too, and some of the most celebrated come from California. Cooper's Hawk Lux Chardonnay is our top-of-the-line dry white wine. Made from Napa Valley grapes, fermented and barrel aged in French oak, Lux Chardonnay is a well-balanced wine, framed in buttery toast and redolent of stone fruit, citrus, pear, almonds, and minerals.

Jackie Raugh

CO-OWNER AND VINTNER
OAKVILLE TERRACES VINEYARD, NAPA, CALIFORNIA

RUSTIC PAELLA

A hearty taste of Spain comes to your table in this festive paella that serves eight to ten hungry diners. If you don't have a traditional paella pan, you will need a similarly large, shallow pan—at least 15 inches in diameter—to hold all of the ingredients. Fruity sangria pairs well with this dish. Just make sure you have enough on hand!

This recipe has been contributed by Napa Valley vintner Jackie Raugh. Jackie and her husband, Gary, have hosted me and other members of the Cooper's Hawk family at their winery and home. The couple purchased their beautiful forty-acre property in 1998, after years of owning and operating smaller vineyards. They now create award-winning wines from their striking vineyard perched in the hills of Oakville overlooking the Napa Valley.

Artfully blending seafood and chicken in a saffron-scented rice, the dish captures the flavors of the Mediterranean. Jackie cooks the shrimp in a traditional style: in the shell with their heads attached. The shells are easy to remove if you like, but many people enjoy eating them. She also calls for Bomba or Calasparra rice, which are slow-maturing Spanish varieties that can absorb up to 30 percent more liquid than most rice found in supermarkets. Fruity sangria pairs well with this paella.

RUSTIC PAELLA

1 tablespoon dried oregano

4 cloves garlic, minced

2 teaspoons freshly ground black
pepper

1½ teaspoons salt

3 tablespoons red wine vinegar

8 tablespoons extra virgin olive oil

4 large boneless chicken breast halves,
preferably skin on (about 2 pounds),
quartered

¼ cup white wine

½ teaspoon saffron threads

1 onion, chopped

3 cups diced fresh tomatoes, or 1 can
(28 ounces) and 1 can (14 ounces)
whole tomatoes, drained and
chopped

2 teaspoons sweet paprika

2 cups short-grain Bomba or Calasparra rice

5 cups homemade or store-bought low-
sodium chicken broth, plus ½ cup
more broth or water if needed

12 large shrimp in the shell with heads
intact

1 cup frozen peas

12 clams, scrubbed

12 mussels, scrubbed and debearded

In a large nonreactive bowl, combine the oregano, half of the garlic, the pepper, 1 teaspoon of the salt, and the vinegar. Whisk in 5 tablespoons of the olive oil, mixing well. Add the chicken and rub it with the marinade in the bowl. Cover the bowl with plastic wrap and refrigerate for at least 8 hours or up to overnight.

In a small saucepan, bring the white wine to a simmer over medium-high heat. Remove the pan from the heat. Crush the saffron between your fingers, dropping it into the hot wine. Stir once or twice and set aside.

In a paella or other large, wide pan, heat the remaining 3 tablespoons olive oil over high heat. Add the chicken and sear on both sides until golden brown, about 3 minutes on each side. Transfer the chicken to a plate and set aside. Reduce the heat to medium, add the onion, and sauté until soft, 3 to 5 minutes. Add the tomatoes, the remaining garlic, and the paprika, mix well, and simmer for 5 minutes. Add the rice, reduce the heat to low, and stir regularly for 2 to 3 minutes.

Raise the heat to high, add the broth, saffron infusion, and the remaining ½ teaspoon salt, and mix well. Bring the liquid to a boil, reduce the heat to low, and cook, uncovered, for 10 minutes. Add the chicken, tucking the pieces into the rice mixture until they are fully covered with the rice. Continue to cook over low heat until all the liquid is absorbed, about 20 minutes. (Do not stir or cover the rice.)

When most of the liquid is absorbed, add the shrimp, carefully tucking them into the rice as you did with the chicken. Sprinkle the peas on top of the rice. Continue to cook over low heat until the shrimp turn pink, about 10 minutes. (If the rice becomes very dry, add another ½ cup broth or water.)

Continue to cook over low heat for 5 more minutes. Remove the pan from the heat and cover to keep warm.

Pour water to a depth of 1 to 2 inches into a large pot and bring to a boil over high heat. Add the clams and mussels, reduce to medium-high heat, and cook until the shellfish open, 3 to 5 minutes. As they open, transfer the shellfish to the paella pan. (Do not mix them into the rice. Just let them sit on top for a great visual effect.) Discard any unopened clams or mussels. Let the paella stand for 10 more minutes before serving.

SERVES 8 TO 10

WINE PROFILE

Cooper's Hawk Red Sangria

Inspired by the traditional fruit-infused wine of Spain, we have blended fresh fruit concentrates with red wine to produce a similarly refreshing and festive sangria. Redolent of oranges, lemons, apples, cherries, and spice, Cooper's Hawk Red Sangria makes a marvelous opener to any meal. And in the spirit of a party, our sangria is wonderful to drink throughout a meal, particularly with a Spanish-themed dish such as paella.

Tim and Dana McEnery

FOUNDERS
COOPER'S HAWK WINERY & RESTAURANTS

ANCHO-AND-POBLANO–BRAISED CHICKEN WITH CORN TORTILLAS

Here's a dish that my wife, Dana, and I enjoy making at home. We often pair it with Cooper's Hawk Red, a versatile wine that goes with many different kinds of food. This dish is colorful and festive, serving up a fine array of textures and tastes. The chicken is only mildly spicy, offering just a hint of heat. Lime juice and cilantro give it a wonderful lightness, but diners won't leave the table hungry! There is plenty to go around.

We use ancho chile powder and poblano chiles (which are simply fresh ancho chiles). But if you can't find one or both, substitute any good chile powder for the ancho chile powder and use Anaheim chiles in place of the poblanos.

ANCHO-AND-POBLANO-BRAISED CHICKEN
WITH CORN TORTILLAS

½ teaspoon ancho chile powder

1 teaspoon garlic powder

1½ teaspoons cumin seeds

¼ teaspoon freshly ground black
  pepper

2 pounds bone-in, skin-on chicken
  thighs (7 or 8 thighs)

½ teaspoon salt

2 tablespoons canola oil

2 small onions, diced

½ poblano or Anaheim chile, seeded
  and finely diced

Kernels from 1 ear corn (about ¾ cup)

1 can (14½ ounces) diced tomatoes,
  with juice

1 cup homemade or store-bought low-
  sodium chicken broth

2 cups brown rice

1 can (14½ ounces) black beans,
  drained and rinsed

10 to 12 corn tortillas, about 6 inches
  in diameter

¼ cup chopped fresh cilantro

2 avocados, halved, pitted, peeled,
  and diced

½ cup crumbled *queso fresco* cheese

2 limes, cut into wedges

In a small bowl, stir together the chile powder, garlic powder, cumin seeds, and black pepper. Rub the mixture on both sides of the chicken thighs. Slip the thighs into a large resealable plastic bag, secure closed, and refrigerate for at least 6 hours or up to overnight.

Preheat the oven to 275°F.

Remove the chicken from the refrigerator and season both sides of the thighs with the salt.

In a large Dutch oven or other large ovenproof pot, heat the canola oil over medium-high heat. Working in batches if necessary to avoid crowding, add the chicken thighs and sear, turning once, until golden brown on both sides, about 3 minutes on each side. Using tongs or a slotted spoon, transfer the chicken to a plate. Set aside.

Reduce the heat to medium, add the onions and chile, and sauté until the onions are translucent, about 5 minutes. Add the corn, mix well, and sauté for 1 minute. Add the tomatoes and their juice and the broth, raise the heat to high, and bring to a low boil. Return the chicken to the pot, tucking the thighs into the liquid.

Cover the pot and transfer it to the oven. Bake, stirring the liquid every 45 minutes, for 2½ hours. Uncover the pot and continue to bake for 30 minutes longer. Remove the pot from the oven, uncovered, and set it on the stove top or on a heatproof surface.

When the chicken has about 40 minutes left to cook in the oven, prepare the brown rice. In a medium pot, bring 4 cups lightly salted water to a boil over high heat. Add the rice, reduce the heat to low, cover, and cook until all the water is absorbed, about 40 minutes. Remove from the heat and set aside covered.

In a small saucepan, heat the black beans over medium-low heat until they are hot. Remove from the heat and cover to keep warm.

The chicken will still be quite hot, so use tongs (or gloves) to shred it. Return the meat to the pot and discard all of the bones and excess skin. Cover the pot and set aside.

To prepare the corn tortillas, heat a medium nonstick skillet over medium-low heat. Add the tortillas, one at a time, and heat, turning once, for 10 seconds on each side. Wrap the tortillas in aluminum foil to keep them warm.

To serve, place a heaping portion of braised chicken in the center of a dinner plate and garnish with the cilantro. Next to the chicken, place a serving of brown rice, a little mound of diced avocado, and a small portion of beans topped with a spoonful of *queso fresco*. Place a lime wedge at the side of the plate. Serve right away. Pass the tortillas at the table.

SERVES 4 TO 6

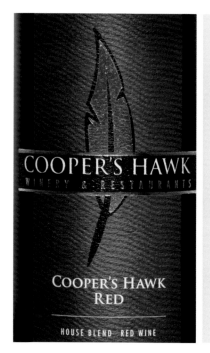

WINE PROFILE

Cooper's Hawk Red

The backbone of our "house red" is a blend of Cabernet Sauvignon and Merlot. This easy-drinking, medium-bodied wine shows off appealing cherry, berry, and spice notes and is styled to mirror its sister wine, Cooper's Hawk White. Like its white counterpart, it is meant to be enjoyed with a broad range of dishes on all kinds of occasions.

DANA'S PARMESAN-CRUSTED CHICKEN WITH TOMATO-BASIL RELISH AND SAUTÉED SPINACH

Here's a recipe created by my wife, Dana. These plump, crunchy-coated chicken breasts are so popular at the restaurants that they have become a signature dish. At the restaurant we serve this dish with a side of creamy mashed potatoes created by my mom, Mary. It's also great with my mother-in-law, Betty's, potatoes. Both recipes can be found in the Basics section (page 183).

On our menu, we have paired this dish with Cooper's Hawk Viognier, a fruity, fresh dry white. But we've also found that guests who enjoy spicier wines like to match Dana's chicken with Cooper's Hawk Shiraz. Both wines are versatile and have wide appeal.

An irresistible golden Parmesan crust frames the tender chicken. (Keep an eye on the stove top. If you leave the chicken in the pan too long, the cheese gets very sticky.) The tomato-basil relish adds a tangy, fresh note and bright color, as does the bed of sautéed spinach.

To shorten your time in the kitchen, ask your butcher to pound the breasts to a thickness of about ¼ inch. If you're doing this at home, use a meat pounder or a rolling pin, being careful not to tear the meat. The pounded breasts become quite wide, so you'll need a very large skillet to cook them (or use two medium-size pans).

No complicated kitchen techniques are required, but you will need to follow a number of steps. Basically, the recipe is four short recipes. Just prepare them in the order that they appear and you'll soon be enjoying one of our favorite dishes.

DANA'S PARMESAN-CRUSTED CHICKEN WITH TOMATO-BASIL RELISH AND SAUTÉED SPINACH

Tomato-Basil Relish

3 cups diced ripe tomatoes (3 or 4 medium tomatoes)

1 tablespoon finely chopped shallot

1 tablespoon finely chopped fresh Italian parsley

¼ cup finely chopped fresh basil

1 clove garlic, minced

2 tablespoons extra virgin olive oil

2 tablespoons fresh lemon juice

Salt and freshly ground black pepper

Mary's Mashed Potatoes (page 185)

Betty's Potatoes (page 186)

To make the relish, in a large bowl, combine all of the ingredients. Using a large spoon, mix thoroughly and set aside.

To prepare the chicken, in a large bowl, combine the bread crumbs, cheese, and parsley. Use a wooden spoon or your hands to mix thoroughly. Put the flour in a shallow bowl. Then, in a medium bowl, whisk the egg whites until frothy. Set the bowls on your work surface.

Cut each chicken breast in half to create 4 fillets total. Lightly season the fillets with salt and pepper. Dredge 1 fillet in the flour, dip it into the egg whites, and then dip it into the bread crumb–cheese mixture, coating thoroughly on both sides. Set it aside on a plate. Repeat with the remaining 3 fillets.

In a large skillet, heat the canola oil and butter over medium-high heat. When the butter has melted, lay the chicken in the pan and cook until a golden brown crust forms on the first side, about 4 minutes. Using a spatula, flip the fillets and cook until the second side is golden brown and the flesh is opaque throughout, about 4 more minutes. Transfer the fillets to a platter, tent with aluminum foil, and set aside.

To cook the spinach, in a medium to large skillet, heat the oil over medium-

Chicken

1 cup *panko* (Japanese bread crumbs)

1 cup grated Parmesan cheese (about 4 ounces)

¼ cup finely chopped fresh Italian parsley

½ cup all-purpose flour

5 egg whites

2 boneless, skinless chicken breasts (about 8 ounces each), pounded ¼ inch thick

Salt and freshly ground black pepper

¼ cup canola oil

1 tablespoon unsalted butter

Spinach

1½ tablespoons extra virgin olive oil

1 clove garlic, minced

½ pound spinach, tough stems removed

Salt and freshly ground black pepper

high heat. When it begins to shimmer, add the garlic. As soon as it starts to brown, after about 15 seconds, add the spinach and stir occasionally just until it starts to wilt. Season to taste with salt and pepper.

To serve, divide the spinach evenly among 4 warmed plates. Set a chicken fillet on top of each spinach portion. Top the chicken with the relish and set a portion of mashed potatoes on the same plate, next to the chicken. Garnish with additional pepper, if desired, and serve right away.

SERVES 4

WINE PROFILE

Cooper's Hawk Shiraz

This easy-drinking wine shows off appealing mixed berry jam notes with a hint of smoke and a peppery finish. Ripe fruit flavors and good acidity form the backbone of this ruby-red blend of mostly Shiraz grapes. A hint of Malbec and Tannat grapes add richness. Toasty oak complements the heat of the ancho and poblano chiles.

Christopher Koetke

EXECUTIVE DIRECTOR
SCHOOL OF CULINARY ARTS, KENDALL COLLEGE
CHICAGO, ILLINOIS

BRAISED CHICKEN PROVENÇAL WITH PAPPARDELLE PASTA

This hearty dish comes to us courtesy of chef Christopher Koetke, executive director of the School of Culinary Arts at Chicago's Kendall College. Koetke has worked in France at such notable restaurants as Le Pavillon Elysée Lenôtre, Pierre Gagnaire, Taillevent, and Pierre Orsi. His love of French cuisine no doubt led him to contribute a recipe that evokes the flavors of southern France. Not surprisingly, the dish marries well with Barbera, a wine varietal from the Piedmont region of Italy, which is next door to Provence. It's also a place where pasta is served at almost every meal.

Rosemary, thyme, and fennel impart their essence to a sauce that generously coats both the pasta and the chicken. If you prefer a lighter version of this dish, trim off the skin from the chicken thighs. Either way, you'll enjoy a heartwarming meal that celebrates the Mediterranean table.

BRAISED CHICKEN PROVENÇAL
WITH PAPPARDELLE PASTA

Grated zest of 1 lemon (about 2
    tablespoons)

Juice of 1 lemon (about 3 table-
    spoons)

Grated zest of 1 orange (about 3½
    tablespoons)

Juice of 1 orange (about ¼ cup)

8 cloves garlic, minced

1 teaspoon fennel seeds

1 teaspoon dried thyme

1½ teaspoons dried rosemary

1 teaspoon salt

½ teaspoon freshly ground black
    pepper

4 pounds chicken thighs (about 10
    thighs)

2 tablespoons extra virgin olive oil

1 large red onion, diced (about 2
    cups)

1 fennel bulb, diced

2 celery stalks, diced (about 1 cup)

8 plum tomatoes, diced

2 cups homemade or store-bought
    low-sodium chicken broth

1 can (8 ounces) tomato sauce

2 teaspoons cornstarch

½ cup pitted Kalamata olives,
    chopped

1 pound dried *pappardelle* or other
    dried thin ribbon pasta noodles

In a large nonreactive bowl, combine the lemon zest and juice, orange zest and juice, garlic, fennel seeds, thyme, rosemary, ½ teaspoon of the salt, and the pepper and mix well. Add the chicken thighs and turn to coat evenly on all sides with the seasoning mixture. Cover and refrigerate for at least 4 hours or up to 8 hours.

Transfer the chicken thighs from the marinade to another bowl, brushing off any large pieces of garlic or zest from the chicken back into the marinade. Reserve the marinade.

In a Dutch oven or other large pot, heat the olive oil over high heat. Working in batches if necessary to avoid crowding, add the chicken thighs and sear, turning once, until browned on both sides, about 3 minutes on each side. Using tongs, transfer the chicken to a clean plate and set aside.

Lower the heat to medium-high, add the onion, fennel, and celery, and sauté until lightly browned, about 5 minutes. Add the tomatoes and cook until they soften, about 3 minutes.

Return the chicken to the pot and mix well with the other ingredients. Add the marinade, broth, tomato sauce, and the remaining ½ teaspoon salt and bring to a boil over high heat. Cover, reduce the heat until the liquid is at a gentle simmer, and cook until the chicken is tender, about 1 hour.

In a medium bowl, mix the cornstarch with 1 tablespoon warm water. Using a large ladle, add 2 scoops of liquid from the pot to the cornstarch mixture and stir well. Return the liquid to the pot and mix well. Continue to simmer the chicken, uncovered, for another 10 minutes to thicken the sauce. Mix in the olives and simmer, uncovered, for 5 to 10 minutes to blend the flavors.

WINE PROFILE

Cooper's Hawk Barbera

With their origin in northern Italy, Barbera grapes provide the core for some of that country's most celebrated wines. Our Barbera is grown in California's Clarksburg district, in the Sacramento Valley, where these juicy, flavorful grapes ripen to perfection. The resulting wine is elegant and leads off with an enticing aromatic note sometimes referred to as "forest floor." These scents blend easily with red-fruit flavors to yield an uncommonly fine dining wine.

Immediately after adding the olives, fill a large pot with lightly salted water and bring to a boil over high heat. Add the pasta and cook until al dente, 5 to 7 minutes or according to package directions. Drain in a colander and shake dry. (Do not rinse with water.)

Divide the pasta among 6 warmed dinner plates or wide, shallow bowls. Top with 1 or 2 pieces of chicken and a generous serving of the sauce. Serve right away.

SERVES 6

Fred LeFranc

RESTAURANT CONSULTANT, STRATEGIST, FOUNDER
RESULTS THRU STRATEGY, INC.
CHARLOTTE, NORTH CAROLINA

HERBED CHICKEN WITH ROSEMARY AND PESTO POTATOES

Recipe contributor Fred LeFranc has vast experience in the restaurant and hospitality industries and has become one of my most trusted advisors. He has run many outstanding restaurants and shares his expertise with entrepreneurs across the nation.

Covered with a crisp brown skin and redolent of herbs and lemon, this rustic roast chicken highlights the complex flavors found in Cooper's Hawk Lux Pinot Noir. The wine serves up just the right amount of herbal notes to match the richly flavored chicken and the crunchy twice-cooked pesto potatoes.

Fred cooks this chicken on a rotisserie. We have adapted his recipe to work in a home oven.

HERBED CHICKEN WITH ROSEMARY
AND PESTO POTATOES

4 tablespoons (½ stick) unsalted but-
　ter, at room temperature
1 tablespoon extra virgin olive oil
2 tablespoons minced fresh rosemary
2 tablespoons minced fresh sage
3 cloves garlic, minced
1 lemon, halved
2 tablespoons white wine
1 whole roasting chicken (about
　5 pounds)
1 onion, halved
1 carrot, coarsely chopped
1 celery stalk, coarsely chopped
1 teaspoon black peppercorns
½ teaspoon sea salt

Potatoes and Pesto
2 pounds Yukon Gold potatoes, halved
　crosswise
1 cup firmly packed fresh basil leaves
¾ cup extra virgin olive oil
2 cloves garlic, chopped
½ cup grated Parmesan cheese
¼ cup pine nuts, toasted (see page
　183)

Preheat the oven to 400°F.

In a small nonreactive bowl, combine the butter, olive oil, rosemary, sage, garlic, juice of ½ lemon, and white wine. Using a wooden spoon, stir to mix well.

Rub the herbed butter mixture over the outside of the chicken and inside the cavity. Insert the onion, carrot, celery, and the remaining ½ lemon into the cavity. Set the prepared chicken on a rack in a roasting pan.

Using a mortar and a pestle or the flat side of a large knife, coarsely crack the peppercorns. Season the outside of the chicken with the cracked pepper and the salt.

Roast until the juices run clear when a thigh joint is poked with a knife or toothpick or an instant-read thermometer inserted into a thigh away from bone registers 165°F, 2 to 2½ hours.

While the chicken is roasting, prepare the potatoes and pesto. In a medium saucepan, combine the potatoes with water to cover and bring to a boil over high heat. Reduce the heat to a simmer and cook until the potatoes can be easily pierced with a fork, about 20 minutes. Drain in a colander and rinse under cold running water. Set aside.

To make the pesto, in a blender, combine the basil leaves, olive oil, and garlic and purée until smooth. Add the cheese and pine nuts and purée until smooth. Pour the pesto into a bowl and set aside. (The pesto can be made up to 3 days in advance, covered, and refrigerated.)

About 20 minutes before the chicken has finished cooking, toss the potatoes in a large bowl with ½ cup of the pesto. (The remaining pesto can be refrigerated for another use.) Arrange the potatoes in a single layer in a small baking pan, place in the oven, and bake until the exteriors are crisp, about 20 minutes. (The pan can be placed in the oven next to the chicken.)

Remove the chicken from the oven and let rest for 5 minutes. Scoop the vegetables out of the cavity and place them on a warmed serving platter or in a warmed bowl. Spoon the potatoes alongside the vegetables. Carve the chicken and arrange on a warmed platter. Scoop off and discard the fat from the pan drippings and spoon the drippings over the chicken, then squeeze the juice from the baked lemon half over the chicken. Serve right away.

SERVES 4

WINE PROFILE

Cooper's Hawk Lux Pinot Noir

As the name implies, this luxuriously styled Pinot Noir shows a pedigree redolent of subtle cherry and herb flavors that unfold slowly but surely along the palate. The layers of flavor are deep and complex. It's made in a distinctly Burgundian style with excellent structure that will please anyone tonight. But it will also age nicely for years to come.

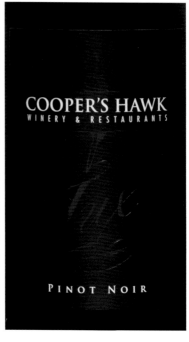

Barry Sorkin
CHEF AND CO-OWNER
SMOQUE BBQ, CHICAGO, ILLINOIS

PORK TACOS WITH GRILLED PINEAPPLE SALSA AND CHILE DE ÁRBOL

This delightful dish was created by Chicago barbecue master Barry Sorkin. Barry started off with a degree in journalism and later entered the world of computer consulting. But his culinary passion led him to follow his heart and open Smoque BBQ, which was named a Bib Gourmand restaurant by the prestigious *MICHELIN Guide* in 2011. Smoque BBQ has also won praise from many other notable publications throughout the nation.

The recipe features an intriguing juxtaposition of flavors. Sweet, smoky pineapple salsa counters the rich, tender pork and spicy chile sauce, bringing a taste of Mexico directly to your table. It's even better when paired with our fruity, off-dry Cooper's Hawk Riesling—a perfect partner for pork.

Chile de árbol, a popular dried Mexican chile, can be found in most supermarkets. The recipe also calls for chipotle chile in adobo sauce. This fiery smoked chile (packed in a tomato and herb sauce) can be purchased in small cans at your local market. Although this recipe is not difficult to prepare, it does call for five separate steps, which are arranged in the order best suited to making the dish. Being well organized is the key to success here.

PORK TACOS WITH GRILLED PINEAPPLE SALSA AND CHILE DE ÁRBOL

Chile de Árbol Sauce

5 pounds ripe tomatoes

3 tablespoons canola oil

10 to 15 *chiles de árbol*

1 onion, quartered

5 cloves garlic, sliced

1 tablespoon salt

Pork

5 pounds boneless pork shoulder,
    trimmed of excess fat and cut into
    1- to 2-inch cubes

Salt and freshly ground black pepper

3 tablespoons canola oil

Grilled Pineapple Salsa

1 ripe pineapple

Salt and freshly ground black pepper

2 tablespoons extra virgin olive oil

Canola oil for coating grill rack

2 roasted red peppers, homemade
    (page 184) or store-bought, cut
    into ¼-inch squares

⅓ cup diced red onion

½ cup minced fresh cilantro

1 chipotle chile in adobo sauce,
    seeded and finely chopped

2 teaspoons fresh lime juice

To Serve

24 corn tortillas, about 8 inches
    diameter

Minced fresh cilantro for garnish

To make the chile sauce, using the tip of a paring knife, cut around the stem of each tomato and remove the core. Set the tomatoes aside.

In a dry medium skillet, heat the canola oil over medium-high heat. Add the chiles and sauté, turning them occasionally, until fragrant, 15 to 20 seconds. Be careful not to burn them or they will turn bitter. Reserve the chiles and the oil.

Fill a large pot half full with water and bring to a boil over high heat. Add the tomatoes, onion, garlic, and chiles and oil and simmer until the tomatoes and onion are soft and the skin on the tomatoes starts to peel, about 10 minutes. Drain in a colander, reserving the solids and discarding the water. When the solids have cooled enough to touch, purée them in batches in a blender or food processor until smooth. Pour the purée into a bowl and remove any large pieces of tomato skin. Add the salt and stir well. Set aside.

To cook the pork, preheat the oven to 350°F. Season the meat on all sides with salt and pepper. In a Dutch oven or a large ovenproof skillet with a tight-fitting lid, heat the canola oil over high heat. Working in batches if necessary to avoid crowding, add the pork and sear, stirring occasionally, until browned on all sides, 2 to 3 minutes on each side.

When all of the meat has been browned, remove the pan from the heat and pour half of the chile sauce over the pork. Cover the remaining sauce and reserve for serving. Cover the pan, transfer it to the oven, and cook, stirring once every hour, until the meat is very tender, 3 to 3½ hours.

Remove the pan from the oven. Using a slotted spoon, remove the largest pieces of meat from the sauce and set them on a carving board. Using tongs or a large fork and knife, coarsely shred the meat and return it to the braising liquid.

While the meat is in the oven, make the pineapple salsa. Prepare a fire in a charcoal or gas grill. Using a sharp knife, cut the skin off of the pineapple. Slice the pineapple lengthwise into ½-inch-thick slabs, cutting around the core. Season the slices lightly on both sides with salt and pepper and brush with the olive oil.

Lightly oil the grill grate with canola oil to prevent sticking. Place the pineapple slices on the grate and grill, turning once, until they are etched with brown grill marks and begin to caramelize, several minutes on each side. Transfer the slices to a cutting board.

When the pineapple slices are cool enough to handle, cut them into ½-inch cubes. In a medium bowl, combine the pineapple, red peppers, onion, cilantro, chipotle chile, and lime juice and toss gently. Taste and add more salt and pepper if needed. Set the salsa aside.

To prepare the corn tortillas, heat a medium nonstick skillet over medium-low heat. Add the tortillas, one at a time, and heat, turning once, for 10 seconds on each side. Wrap the tortillas in aluminum foil to keep them warm until serving.

For each taco, place 2 tortillas, one on top of the other, on a warmed dinner plate. Using a slotted spoon, place a large scoop of meat in the center of the top tortilla. Place a spoonful of the pineapple salsa over the meat. Drizzle with the reserved chile sauce. Garnish with the cilantro and serve.

MAKES 12 TACOS; SERVES 6

WINE PROFILE

Cooper's Hawk Riesling

Pleasant peach, citrus, and spice flavors are at the core of this refreshing off-dry wine, made with grapes from Washington. It's not too sweet and can pair beautifully with both savory and sweeter dishes. Matched with Barry Sorkin's spicy pork and pineapple salsa, Riesling doesn't get much better! The wine is also fabulous on its own as an aperitif.

Ursula Korus

**DIRECTOR OF WINE CLUB AND RESTAURANT MARKETING
COOPER'S HAWK WINERY & RESTAURANTS**

MEDITERRANEAN POT ROAST WITH PAPPARDELLE PASTA

Rich and hearty, this dish has great chunks of firm-textured meat at its core. It was created by Ursula Korus, winner of the first Cooper's Hawk Recipe Challenge in July 2011. For this event, twenty-five contestants submitted an original recipe using the wine of the month and then prepared their recipe for the judges. Not only were we smitten with Ursula's amazing pot roast, but we were also smitten with Ursula, who was not working for Cooper's Hawk at the time. Two months after her triumph in the kitchen, Ursula became part of the Cooper's Hawk marketing team.

Dried figs give this dish a special touch, adding just a hint of sweetness that's balanced by tangy olives and—of course—a fine, dry red wine like Cooper's Hawk Tempranillo. Ursula likes to serve her pot roast over potatoes, pasta, or gnocchi. Here, we have opted for thin, wide *pappardelle* noodles, which cook a little faster than many thicker noodles. She calls for Manchego cheese, a sharp, aged Spanish sheep's milk cheese. If you can't find it, Parmesan or a sharp white English Cheddar is a good substitute.

MEDITERRANEAN POT ROAST WITH PAPPARDELLE PASTA

2 pounds beef top round roast, cut into 3 uniform pieces

10 cloves garlic, halved lengthwise

2 ounces pancetta, cut into 20 equal pieces

2 cups Cooper's Hawk Tempranillo or other dry red wine

Salt and freshly ground black pepper

2 to 3 tablespoons extra virgin olive oil

1 parsnip, peeled and diced

4 celery stalks, diced

2 carrots, peeled and diced

1 white onion, minced

3 tablespoons tomato paste

2 cups homemade or store-bought low-sodium beef broth

6 to 8 dried figs, diced

15 pitted medium-size green olives, diced

1 pound dried *pappardelle* pasta

½ cup grated Manchego cheese

4 teaspoons minced fresh chives

Using the tip of a paring knife, make 40 small incisions, each about ½ inch deep, all over the meat. Insert ½ garlic clove in every other incision, alternating with 1 piece of pancetta, until all of the garlic and pancetta have been inserted.

Set the roast in a glass or porcelain bowl and pour the red wine over it. Cover and marinate in the refrigerator for at least 8 hours or up to overnight. If the wine doesn't cover the meat, flip the meat at the midway point of marination.

Remove the meat from the wine and reserve the wine. Pat the meat dry with paper towels and season with salt and pepper. In a Dutch oven or other large, heavy pot, heat 2 tablespoons of the olive oil over medium-high heat until it shimmers. Add the meat and sear on all four sides until browned, 2 to 3 minutes on each side. Transfer the meat to a plate and set aside. Turn off the heat but leave the pot on the stove.

Using a food processor or blender, coarsely grind together the parsnip, celery, carrots, and onion. Be careful not to liquefy them. There should still be enough oil remaining in the pot to sauté the vegetables. If the surface appears dry, add another tablespoon. Turn on the heat to medium. When the oil is hot, add the ground vegetables and cook, stirring occasionally, until they begin to brown, about 15 minutes. Add the tomato paste, ½ teaspoon salt, and pepper to taste and stir to mix thoroughly.

Add the reserved wine and the broth to the pot, raise the heat to high, and bring to a boil. Return the meat to the pot, lower the heat to a gentle simmer, cover, and cook for 1 hour, stirring occasionally. Flip the meat after 30 minutes.

After the meat has cooked for 1 hour, uncover the pot and continue to simmer for another 30 minutes. Remove the meat from the pot and slice into thin strips about 1 inch long. Return the sliced meat to the pot and add the figs and olives. Mix thoroughly and let simmer, uncovered, until the sauce thickens, about 30 more minutes. Taste and add more salt and pepper if needed.

When the pot roast is almost done, fill a large pot with lightly salted water and bring to a boil over high. Add the pasta and cook until al dente, 5 to 7 minutes or according to package directions. (If the water starts to splatter, reduce the heat slightly but maintain a boil.) Drain the pasta in a colander and shake dry.

Divide the pasta equally among 4 to 6 warmed plates and top with a generous portion of meat and sauce. Garnish with the cheese and chives and serve immediately.

SERVES 4 TO 6

WINE PROFILE

Cooper's Hawk Tempranillo

October 2012 Wine of the Month
Tempranillo is the classic red grape of Spain's Rioja region. It also grows well in California's Sacramento Valley Clarksburg district, where Cooper's Hawk sources grapes. This is a medium-bodied red wine that offers hints of plum, cherry, and spice, all framed in soft, ripe tannins. It's perfect with poultry and meats, especially the pot roast featured here.

Gary Baca

EXECUTIVE CHEF AND VICE PRESIDENT
JOE'S SEAFOOD, PRIME STEAK & STONE CRAB
CHICAGO, ILLINOIS

BRAISED BEEF SHORT RIBS WITH VEAL DEMI-GLACE

These beef short ribs are easy to prepare. But they are so impressive to behold that your dinner guests will assume you've spent hours in the kitchen. The recipe was given to us by our friend Gary Baca, a California native who has brought a culinary ray of West Coast sunshine to the Windy City.

Gary realized his passion for cooking at a young age while spending time with his grandmothers, both of whom taught him valuable lessons in the kitchen. After graduating from Santa Barbara City College's Culinary Arts program, Gary established himself at a number of fine restaurants and as a corporate consultant, eventually moving east to Chicago. Today, Gary's role as executive chef is to guarantee that the integrity of the original Joe's Stone Crab of South Miami Beach is maintained in its branches in both Chicago and Las Vegas.

The slow-cooked meat in this dish is so tender that it falls off the bone. Drenched in a veal demi-glace (available in most specialty food stores), it offers carnivores a wonderfully hedonistic experience enhanced by a great glass of wine—in this case a big, bold Cooper's Hawk Petite Sirah. For a full-blown main course, serve with Mary's Mashed Potatoes (page 185).

5 pounds beef short ribs, trimmed of
  excess fat
Salt and freshly ground black pepper
1 onion, coarsely chopped
2 cloves garlic, minced
3 carrots, peeled and cut into 1-inch
  pieces
2 celery stalks, cut into ¼-inch pieces
1 teaspoon dried thyme
1 teaspoon dried oregano
1 bay leaf
½ teaspoon black peppercorns
3 cups red wine
1½ cups veal demi-glace concentrate
3 tablespoons extra virgin olive oil
3 tablespoons tomato paste

Season the ribs on both sides with salt and pepper and set aside.

In a very large bowl, combine the onion, garlic, carrots, celery, thyme, oregano, bay leaf, peppercorns, and red wine and mix thoroughly. Add the short ribs, cover, and marinate for 2 to 3 hours at room temperature. Meanwhile, prepare the veal demi-glace. In a medium pot, bring 6 cups water to a boil over high heat. Remove the pot from the heat and add the demi-glace concentrate, whisking to incorporate with the water. Set aside.

Preheat the oven to 350°F.

In a Dutch oven or large, deep ovenproof pan, heat the olive oil over medium-high heat until it begins to shimmer. Using tongs, remove the ribs from the marinade. Working in batches if necessary to avoid crowding, add the ribs and sear, turning once, until browned on both sides, about 3 minutes total. Transfer the ribs to a large plate or bowl and set aside. Leave the oil in the pan.

Using a slotted spoon, remove the vegetables from the marinade. Add the vegetables to the pan and sauté over medium heat until the onion is translucent, 5 to 7 minutes. Add the wine from the marinade, the tomato paste, and ½ teaspoon salt and mix well. Raise the heat to medium-high and bring the liquid to a gentle boil. Lower the heat to medium and simmer until the wine is reduced by half, about 10 minutes.

Return the meat to the pan. Stir the veal demi-glace to give it an even consistency and pour it over the meat, adding just enough to come three-fourths of the way up the sides of the meat. (Reserve the remainder for another use.) Cover the pan, transfer to the oven, and cook until the meat is fork-tender, 3 to 3½ hours. To thicken the sauce, uncover the pan for the last 30 to 45 minutes of cooking.

SERVES 6

Braised Beef Short Ribs with Veal
Demi-Glace, page 150

Cooper's Hawk
Petite Sirah

The deep red of this wine lets us
know that it has an intense flavor
before we even drink it. It kicks off
with smoky, toasty aromas followed by hints of dark cherry. On
the palate, it is full bodied, rich,
and lushly textured with gorgeous
black-fruit flavors ranging from more
cherries to blackberries and cassis.
This is the kind of wine that can
easily stand up to rich red-meat
dishes, including, of course, these
fork-tender short ribs.

CHIMICHURRI SKIRT STEAK WITH FRESH CORN, GREEN BEAN, AND BACON HASH

Lean skirt steaks take on an exotic note when marinated in the South American–inspired *chimichurri* sauce shared with us by chef Randy Zweiban, whose Latin-inspired cuisine is acclaimed in Chicago and throughout the United States. Randy's keen sense of style in the kitchen was fine-tuned in Miami, where he worked prior to coming to Chicago. He is also a talented musician who has performed in New York. Province earned three stars from the *Chicago Tribune*, and Randy is continually featured in publications across the nation.

Make sure you don't leave the steaks on the grill too long. The meat pairs well with the smoky, sweet, earthy flavors in the hash and with the herb, cocoa, and coffee notes in our Cooper's Hawk Lux Cabernet Sauvignon.

Randy typically uses pork belly—essentially uncured bacon—for this dish. We've taken the liberty of using bacon here to simplify your shopping list and your time in the kitchen.

CHIMICHURRI SKIRT STEAK WITH FRESH CORN, GREEN BEAN, AND BACON HASH

Chimichurri Sauce

½ cup extra virgin olive oil

½ cup chopped fresh basil

¼ cup chopped fresh cilantro

1 teaspoon minced onion

1 teaspoon white wine vinegar

1 teaspoon minced, seeded jalapeño
  chile

½ teaspoon ground cumin

½ teaspoon honey

4 skirt steaks, 6 to 8 ounces each

2 tablespoons mayonnaise, homemade
  (page 183) or store-bought

1 clove garlic, minced

⅛ teaspoon cayenne pepper

2½ cups corn kernels (from 3 to 4 ears
  corn)

2½ cups cut-up green beans (2-inch
  lengths)

1 tablespoon extra virgin olive oil

4 slices bacon, diced

To make the *chimichurri* sauce, in a blender or food processor, combine the olive oil, basil, cilantro, onion, vinegar, chile, cumin, and honey and purée until smooth. Transfer the sauce to a small bowl and set aside.

Prick each steak on both sides several times with the tines of a fork and arrange the steaks in a single layer on a large platter. Using a few tablespoons of the sauce, brush the sauce on both sides of each steak, then let the steaks sit, uncovered, at room temperature for about 45 minutes prior to grilling. Reserve the remaining sauce for serving.

Prepare a medium-hot fire in a charcoal or gas grill.

In a small bowl, stir together the mayonnaise, garlic, and cayenne pepper. Cover and refrigerate until ready to use.

Heat a large skillet over medium-high heat. When the pan is very hot, add the corn kernels and sear, stirring frequently with a wooden spoon to prevent burning, until golden brown, about 5 minutes. Transfer the corn to a medium bowl and set aside. Turn off the heat but leave the pan on the stove top for use later.

Pour water to a depth of 3 inches into a small pot and bring to a boil over high heat. Add the green beans and cook until crisp tender, 2 to 3 minutes. Drain the beans in a colander and rinse under cold running water. Set aside.

If necessary, scrape away any browned bits of corn that may be stuck to the skillet. Then add the olive oil to the skillet and heat over medium-high heat.

When the oil is hot, add the bacon and cook until browned and crisp, about 4 minutes. Add the green beans and sauté, stirring occasionally, for 1 minute. Stir in the corn and sauté for 1 minute longer. Transfer to a medium bowl and stir in the seasoned mayonnaise, mixing well. Cover to keep warm.

When the fire is ready, place the steaks on the grill grate and cook for 2 minutes on the first side. Flip the steaks and cook for 1 minute longer on the second side for medium-rare or 2 minutes for medium. Remove the steaks from the grill and let them rest for a few minutes before serving.

Place a mound of the corn hash in the middle of each warmed dinner plate and lean a steak against the hash. Spoon a teaspoon or two of the remaining *chimichurri* sauce on each steak. Serve right away.

SERVES 4

Evan Goldstein
MASTER SOMMELIER
FULL CIRCLE SOLUTIONS, SAN FRANCISCO, CALIFORNIA

TOP SIRLOIN WITH MASALA RUB, SHIITAKE MUSHROOM RISOTTO, AND BROCCOLINI

Master Sommelier Evan Goldstein comes by his love of food honestly. His mother, Joyce, is one of America's best-known chefs and cookbook authors. (Joyce has also contributed a recipe to this book on page 163.) Evan worked with Joyce at Square One restaurant in San Francisco, which she ran for more than a decade, ending in 1996. Currently, he owns and operates Full Circle Solutions, a wine and spirits education firm that specializes in hospitality training.

Several years ago, Evan traveled through the southern Indian state of Kerala and found himself profoundly influenced by the exotic aromas and flavors of the region. Some of those qualities are mirrored in our spicy, fruity Cooper's Hawk Syrah.

For this recipe, a tender top sirloin roast is seasoned with a simple masala, a fragrant blend of spices that varies depending on its region of origin. The core elements typically include coriander, cardamom, cinnamon, cloves, cumin, nutmeg, ginger, and black pepper. Evan recommends looking for a commercial blend from a reputable producer. These and other brands can be found in many supermarkets. Look for bottles labeled masala or garam masala.

TOP SIRLOIN WITH MASALA RUB, SHIITAKE MUSHROOM RISOTTO, AND BROCCOLINI

Roast

1 teaspoon salt

1½ tablespoons masala or garam masala

1 top sirloin roast (about 4½ pounds)

Risotto

3 tablespoons extra virgin olive oil

1 onion, minced

2 cloves garlic, minced

4 ounces shiitake mushrooms, trimmed and diced

1 cup Arborio rice

4 cups homemade or store-bought low-sodium chicken broth, plus more if needed

1 cup red wine

⅓ cup grated Parmesan cheese

Salt and freshly ground black pepper

Broccolini

1 pound broccolini, ends trimmed

¼ cup extra virgin olive oil

½ lemon

Salt and freshly ground black pepper

To cook the roast, in a small bowl, use a fork or whisk to mix together the salt and masala. Using your hands, thoroughly rub the spices into the meat. Let sit at room temperature for about 1 hour. (Do not trim the meat of excess fat.)

Preheat the oven to 425°F.

Place the roast on a rack in a roasting pan and cook for 25 minutes. Reduce the heat to 325°F and cook until an instant-read thermometer inserted into the center of the roast registers about 135°F for medium-rare. Plan on 15 to 20 minutes per pound, depending on the effectiveness of your oven, or about 1 hour after the heat has been lowered.

When the roast is ready, transfer it to a carving board, tent with aluminum foil, and let rest for about 30 minutes before carving.

To make the risotto, in a large, heavy skillet, heat the olive oil over medium-high heat. Add the onion and garlic and sauté until they are translucent, about 3 minutes. Reduce the heat to medium, push the onion and garlic to the side of the pan, and add the mushrooms. Cover the pan and cook until the mushrooms are wilted, about 10 minutes. Add the rice and stir thoroughly with a wooden spoon until it is evenly coated with the oil. Add the broth ½ cup at a time alternately with the wine ½ cup at a time, stirring after each addition just until the liquid has been absorbed. When all of the wine has been incorporated, continue adding the broth, ½ cup at a time and stirring after each addition, until the rice kernels are tender but still slightly firm in the center, about 30 minutes. If necessary, add more broth to cook the rice.

Remove from the heat, add the Parmesan, and mix well. Season to taste with salt and pepper and keep warm.

Just before the risotto is ready, begin cooking the broccolini. Pour water to a depth of 2 inches into a large skillet or sauté pan and bring to a rapid boil over high heat. Place the broccolini in the water and reduce the heat to a simmer. Cook until tender crisp, about 5 minutes.

Drain in a colander and transfer to a serving bowl. Drizzle the olive oil over the hot broccolini, then squeeze the juice of the lemon half over the top. Season with salt and pepper, then toss gently to coat the broccolini evenly with the oil and lemon juice.

Carve the roast against the grain into ½-inch-thick slices and arrange on a warmed platter. Serve immediately with the risotto and broccolini.

SERVES 4 TO 6

WINE PROFILE

Cooper's Hawk Syrah

In the Rhône Valley of southern France, Syrah is the king of red grapes. It is known for its earthy edge and spiced fruity notes. Cooper's Hawk Syrah, which is made from Washington State grapes, has a deep, dark color and serves up an intriguing mix of coffee, cola, and chocolate flavors—as intriguing as the aromas found in the masala rub used in the accompanying recipe. The wine is full bodied, richly textured, and also shows off a touch of gaminess for added interest.

Joyce Goldstein
COOKBOOK AUTHOR AND CHEF
SAN FRANCISCO, CALIFORNIA

LAMB TAGINE WITH PRUNES AND HONEY

Renowned chef and cookbook author Joyce Goldstein offers us this marvelous recipe adapted from her book, *Saffron Shores: Jewish Cooking of the Southern Mediterranean* (Chronicle Books, 2002).

For more than a decade, Joyce owned and operated her Mediterranean-themed restaurant, Square One, in San Francisco, which she closed in 1996. Since then, she has written a remarkable collection of cookbooks while pursuing a culinary path that keeps her cooking around the globe.

This Algerian-inspired *tagine,* or stew, delivers an exotic blend of flavors, most notably coriander, cinnamon, saffron, and ginger, that conjures up the heady aromas of Northern Africa. Prunes and honey give a hint of sweetness, which pairs beautifully with Cooper's Hawk Lux Meritage. The stew is served atop a mound of light-textured couscous—easy to make and perfectly suited to the dish.

Joyce tells us that this recipe is traditionally served on the second night of the Jewish new year, Rosh Hashanah, when sweet foods are eaten to symbolize a sweet new year. If desired, beef can be substituted for the lamb.

LAMB TAGINE WITH PRUNES AND HONEY

8 ounces pitted prunes (about 2 cups)

2½ tablespoons extra virgin olive oil

2 pounds boneless lamb shoulder, cut into 1- to 2-inch cubes

1½ onions, chopped

¾ teaspoon ground cinnamon

½ teaspoon ground ginger

1 teaspoon ground coriander

⅛ teaspoon saffron threads

¼ teaspoon freshly ground black pepper

2 cups homemade or store-bought low-sodium beef broth

2 tablespoons honey

1 teaspoon salt

2 tablespoons sesame seeds

1½ cups couscous

In a medium bowl, combine the prunes with warm water to cover and soak until plumped, about 1 hour.

Meanwhile, in a Dutch oven or other large, heavy pot, heat 2 tablespoons of the olive oil over medium heat. Working in batches if necessary to avoid crowding, add the lamb and sear until browned on all sides, about 3 minutes on each side. Using a slotted spoon, transfer to a plate and set aside.

Add the onions to the pot and sauté over medium heat until tender, about 5 minutes. Stir in the cinnamon, ginger, coriander, saffron, and pepper and cook, stirring, for about 1 minute. Return the browned lamb to the pot and add the broth, stirring gently. Raise the heat to high and bring the liquid to a boil. Reduce the heat to a simmer, cover, and cook for 45 minutes.

Drain the prunes, add them to the stew, and re-cover the pot. Continue to simmer until the meat is tender, another 20 minutes longer. Uncover, stir in the honey and ½ teaspoon of the salt, and continue to cook over medium-high heat until the sauce thickens slightly, about 10 minutes.

While the meat is finishing cooking, toast the sesame seeds and prepare the couscous. In a small, dry skillet, toast the sesame seeds over medium heat, stirring steadily to prevent burning, until fragrant, 2 to 3 minutes. Transfer immediately to a plate or bowl and let cool. Set aside.

Pour the couscous into a glass baking dish. In a medium saucepan, bring 2½ cups water to a boil over high heat and add the remaining ½ teaspoon salt and ½ tablespoon oil. Remove from the heat and slowly pour the boiling water over the couscous while mixing with a fork to keep the grains moist and to prevent clumping. Cover the baking dish with plastic wrap and set aside for 10 minutes. Just before serving, fluff the couscous with a fork.

To serve, place a generous portion of couscous in the middle of each warmed dinner plate and top with the lamb *tagine*. Garnish with the toasted sesame seeds and serve right away.

SERVES 4

WINE PROFILE

Cooper's Hawk Lux Meritage

The term *meritage* refers to wines made using a blend of the traditional Bordeaux varietals. This red wine is made from Merlot, Malbec, Petit Verdot, and Cabernet Sauvignon grapes, which together yield a beautifully complex array of flavors. Cooper's Hawk winemaker Rob Warren says, "This is the winemaker's opportunity to make the best of the best. There is a reason Bordeaux is so famous; these grapes work extremely well together."

This wine is quite aromatic, showing beautiful spice, plum, and herb notes upfront. Framed in toasty oak with ripe tannins, the flavors spread out with precision across the tongue. Anise, blackberry, cassis, coffee, and thyme come to mind with a finish that ends long and luxuriously.

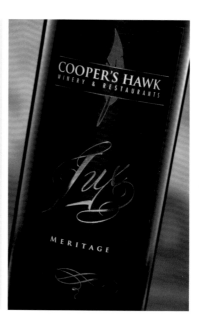

Gale Gand

**EXECUTIVE PASTRY CHEF AND PARTNER
TRU, CHICAGO, ILLINOIS**

BUTTERMILK PANNA COTTA WITH HIBISCUS-INFUSED BERRIES

This creamy Italian-inspired custard comes to us courtesy of Gale Gand, whose resume reads like a chef's dream. She is executive pastry chef and a partner at the renowned Tru restaurant in Chicago. She was named among *Food & Wine* magazine's Top 10 Best New Chefs in 1994, and in 2001, she was winner of the James Beard Award for Outstanding Pastry Chef. In her spare time she has written seven cookbooks, become a Food Channel television personality, and appeared on numerous other television shows. Gale has opened a number of other restaurants as well—all this while raising three marvelous children. Just to keep things lively, she also runs Gale's Root Beer, a company that makes this much-loved drink in a truly artisanal manner, with notes of cinnamon, ginger, and vanilla.

Gale's buttermilk *panna cotta* is guaranteed to please both adults and children. It hits just the right notes after a meal, with a light-textured creaminess and an elegant sweetness. The hibiscus-infused fruit tops the dish with bright, fresh color.

Enjoy our equally elegant, sweet yet refreshing Cooper's Hawk Moscato, the perfect accompaniment for this first-rate finale.

Panna Cotta

1½ cups heavy cream

½ cup plus 2 tablespoons sugar

½ vanilla bean (about 3 inches long),
    split lengthwise

2 teaspoons powdered gelatin

2 cups buttermilk

Infused Berries

1 hibiscus tea bag

½ cup sugar

½ cup strawberries, hulled and diced

½ cup raspberries, halved

To make the *panna cotta*, in a saucepan, whisk together the cream, the sugar, and vanilla bean over medium heat, whisking until the sugar dissolves. When the liquid begins to boil, reduce the heat to low.

While the cream-sugar mixture is heating up, prepare the gelatin. Put 5 teaspoons cold water in a small bowl and sprinkle in the gelatin. (The gelatin will absorb all of the water within 1 to 2 minutes.) Using a rubber spatula, scrape the gelatin out of the bowl and into the hot cream. Using the whisk, incorporate the gelatin into the liquid. Add the buttermilk and continue to whisk over low heat for 1 minute. Do not allow the mixture to boil.

Remove the saucepan from the heat. Strain the cream mixture through a fine-mesh sieve into a medium pitcher or bowl. Discard the vanilla bean. Pour or ladle the strained cream into six 4-inch ramekins, filling them to the rim. Refrigerate until firm, about 4 hours. After the custard has set, cover each ramekin with plastic wrap and return to the refrigerator until ready to serve.

To make the infused berries, bring ½ cup water to a boil and pour it into a tea or coffee cup. Add the tea bag and let steep for 3 minutes. Discard the bag.

In a small saucepan, combine 1 cup water, the sugar, and the hibiscus tea. Bring to a boil over high heat, stirring occasionally until the sugar has dissolved. Remove from the heat and let cool to room temperature, about 30 minutes. Pour the syrup into a bowl and add the strawberries and raspberries. Cover and refrigerate for at least 1 hour or up to 12 hours before serving.

To serve, top each ramekin with a spoonful of the infused berries.

SERVES 6

Buttermilk Panna Cotta with Hibiscus-Infused Berries, page 166

WINE PROFILE

Cooper's Hawk Moscato

The flavors of honey and peach are at the center of this stylish dessert wine. Made from traditional Moscato (or Muscat) grapes, it's sweet, but not too sweet to enjoy on its own as an aperitif. Bright acidity adds finesse and keeps it fresh on the palate. It also pairs beautifully here for dessert alongside Gale Gand's silky *panna cotta* crowned with hibiscus-infused strawberries and raspberries.

SUMMER SHORTCAKE WITH PEACHES AND BERRIES

"This is one of my favorite desserts," says Cooper's Hawk chef Matt McMillin. "I serve it all summer and change up the fruits as they ripen through the months."

Matt came to Cooper's Hawk after working extensively in French- and Asian-themed restaurants and is the coauthor of *Big Bowl Noodles and Rice,* a collection of home-style Asian recipes. He has cooked professionally since he was in his early twenties and says, "If I could cook for twenty-four hours a day, I would!" Matt has brought his passion for cooking to Cooper's Hawk, where he is responsible for creating and fine-tuning our menu items.

A great meal also involves certain artistic intangibles, however. "One lesson I learned while I was young," Matt notes, "is the importance of cooking from the heart. No matter what you are working on, it can always be made with love. That's what makes food taste great!"

This light-textured blend of fresh fruit is surrounded by fluffy whipped cream, all neatly sandwiched in a soft, flaky, buttery shortcake.

Enjoy with a chilled glass of Cooper's Hawk Ice Wine.

SUMMER SHORTCAKE WITH PEACHES AND BERRIES

Shortcakes

4 tablespoons (½ stick) unsalted butter, cut into small cubes

1½ cups all-purpose flour, plus more
   for dusting

4 teaspoons granulated sugar

2½ teaspoons baking powder

2½ teaspoons salt

¾ cup plus 2 tablespoons heavy cream

Peach-Berry Mix

3 cups thinly sliced yellow peaches

1 cup blueberries

Chopped zest of 1 orange (about 2
   tablespoons)

Juice of 1 orange (about ¼ cup)

1 tablespoon granulated sugar

½ cup blackberries

½ cup raspberries

Whipped Cream

1 cup heavy cream

½ teaspoon vanilla extract

1 tablespoon confectioners' sugar

2 tablespoons confectioners' sugar for
   dusting

6 small fresh mint sprigs for garnish

To make the shortcakes, preheat the oven to 350°F. Line a baking sheet with parchment paper. Place the diced butter in a small bowl and set in the freezer until very cold, about 10 minutes.

While the butter is chilling, in a large bowl, sift or stir together the flour, 2½ teaspoons of the granulated sugar, the baking powder, and the salt.

Dust your hands with flour and, using your fingers, mix the cold butter into the flour mixture until it resembles coarse cornmeal. Using a wooden spoon (or your fingers), slowly stir in ¾ cup of the cream. If necessary, dust the spoon with flour to prevent sticking. Do not overmix; the dough should be smooth but not sticky. After 2 or 3 minutes, the mixture will have come together in a stretchy ball of dough.

Lightly flour a work surface. Dust your hands again with flour and set the dough on the floured surface. Using a rolling pin, roll out the dough into a 9-by-6-inch rectangle 1 inch thick. Using a sharp knife, cut the dough into 6 cakes each about 3 inches square. Place the squares on the prepared baking sheet. Brush the tops of the shortcakes with the remaining 2 tablespoons cream, then dust with the remaining 1½ teaspoons granulated sugar.

Bake the shortcakes, rotating the baking sheet back to front after 12 minutes, until they begin to turn golden, about 25 minutes. Remove from the oven and let cool on the pan on a wire rack.

To make the peach-berry mix, in a medium bowl, combine the peaches, blueberries, orange zest, orange juice, and granulated sugar. Mix gently with a spoon and set aside at room temperature for at least 1 hour or up to 3 hours. Just before serving, mix in the blackberries and raspberries.

Just before serving, make the whipped cream. In a medium bowl, combine the cream, vanilla, and confectioners' sugar. Using an electric mixer or a whisk, beat the cream mixture until stiff peaks form. Set aside.

To assemble the dessert, using a sharp knife, carefully cut each shortcake in half horizontally, making "sandwich" halves. Place the bottom half of each shortcake, cut side up, on an individual dessert plate. Spoon an equal amount of the fruit mixture on each shortcake bottom. Top the fruit with a dollop of whipped cream. Gently place the shortcake tops, cut side down, on top of the whipped cream. Using a fine-mesh sieve, dust the tops of the shortcakes with the confectioners' sugar, then garnish each cake with a mint sprig. Serve right away.

SERVES 6

Cooper's Hawk Ice Wine

This wine is made with Vidal Blanc, a hybrid grape developed by crossing the European *vinifera* grape species and the American *labrusca* grape species. Its American roots make it hardy enough to withstand the cold winters common to Canada and neighboring Michigan, where the grapes for this wine are grown. Grapes for ice wine are harvested in midwinter, long after the leaves have dropped off the vines. The frozen grapes still have a sweet, syrupy core that is slowly pressed and then fermented to create one of the most exquisite dessert wines on the planet. This wine is syrupy smooth, lush textured, and redolent of honey, stone fruit, spice, and apricots. It also has great acidity, which provides fine-tuned balance and structure. After dinner, we can't think of a better accompaniment for chef Matt McMillin's Summer Shortcake with Peaches and Berries. Dessert doesn't get much better!

Ryan Hutmacher

CHEF, COFOUNDER, AND CEO
CENTERED CHEF, CHICAGO, ILLINOIS

COCONUT RICE PUDDING WITH RUM-SPICED MANGOES

If you like coconut, you'll love this creamy coconut dessert that blends the flavors of the Caribbean and Italy. The dish is brought to us by chef Ryan Hutmacher, who, when he's not cooking up tasty, healthful treats, excels as a triathlete dedicated to raising awareness about health and wellness through sports and nutrition.

Arborio rice, the classic short-grain risotto rice, gives this dish an unique texture that combines chewy and crunchy notes. Topped with mangoes laced with fresh mint, the pudding is rich and sweet yet refreshing— the perfect ending for a special meal with friends that includes a bottle of Cooper's Hawk Holiday Red.

You can make the mango topping in about fifteen minutes. Prepare it before you make the pudding, then refrigerate it until ready to use; it will keep for up to eight hours. But if you are serving the pudding warm or at room temperature, you can also make the topping after the pudding has cooked or even while it is cooking.

Mango Topping

1/2 tablespoon fresh lime juice

1 1/2 tablespoons firmly packed brown sugar

1 teaspoon dark rum

1 ripe mango, pitted, peeled, and cut into 1-inch cubes (about 2 1/2 cups)

1/2 tablespoon minced fresh mint

Pudding

1 can (14 ounces) unsweetened coconut milk

1/4 cup sugar

1/4 cup unsweetened shredded dried coconut

1/3 cup Arborio rice

1/8 teaspoon salt

1/4 teaspoon vanilla extract

To make the mango topping, in a medium nonreactive bowl, stir together the lime juice, brown sugar, and rum. Add the mango and mint and stir gently to coat evenly. Set aside for at least 10 minutes or cover and refrigerate for up to 8 hours.

To make the pudding, in a medium saucepan, combine the coconut milk, 1 cup water, the sugar, coconut, rice, and salt and bring to a gentle boil over medium-high heat, stirring frequently. Reduce the heat to low, cover partially, and simmer until most of the liquid is absorbed, about 30 minutes. You will need to scrape the sides and bottom of the pan with a heat-resistant spatula occasionally to prevent burning. The pudding will ultimately thicken to a loose, oatmeal-like consistency. Remove from the heat and stir in the vanilla extract.

Divide the pudding evenly among 4 individual dessert bowls. It can be served hot, or you can let it sit at room temperature for 2 or 3 hours before serving. It can also be covered and refrigerated for up to 3 days and served cold.

To serve, spoon the mango topping on top of the pudding.

SERVES 4

Coconut Rice Pudding with
Rum-Spiced Mangoes, page 174

Cooper's Hawk Holiday Red

Who needs mistletoe when you have a glass of our Holiday Red? It smells just like Christmas, with apple pie and cinnamon notes steeped in mulled spices. In the winter, we heat it and serve it warm with an orange slice balanced on the rim of the glass. If you weren't sipping it, you would swear you are biting into a piece of apple pie—it is dessert in a glass. But it is also superb served alongside this coconut-flavored rice pudding.

Larry Binstein

**VICE PRESIDENT OF SALES AND MARKETING
EUROPEAN IMPORTS, LTD., CHICAGO, ILLINOIS**

APRICOT-ALMOND TART WITH THREE CHEESES

European Imports, Ltd. is a longtime partner of Cooper's Hawk, providing cheeses for monthly cheese tastings and specialty food products for our kitchens. The company was founded by Larry Binstein's parents in 1978, and it remains a family affair today, with Larry and his two brothers, Jeff and Glenn, working together with their parents.

In this recipe, Larry makes excellent use of almond paste to create a tantalizing tart that looks like something you would find in a fine Parisian patisserie. It's not too sweet, which makes it an excellent match for the three cheeses suggested as an accompaniment to the tart—all complemented by a glass of luscious Cooper's Hawk Nightjar, made in the style of Port.

The three cheeses are Spanish Manchego, a nutty, aged sheep cheese with an attractively briny edge; Monte Enebro, a creamy, tangy Spanish goat cheese that sports a salty ash rind and a mineral-like edge; and Fourme d'Ambert, a rich, buttery cow's milk blue from central France with a seductive earthiness. If you can't find these exact cheeses, look for similarly styled ones to accompany the tart. And if you wish to forgo the cheese, the tart is quite tasty on its own, too!

APRICOT-ALMOND TART WITH THREE CHEESES

Crust

½ cup (1 stick) plus 1 tablespoon
    unsalted butter, at room temperature

⅓ cup sugar

1 egg

1 cup all-purpose flour, plus more for
    kneading

½ teaspoon salt

Filling

⅓ cup almond paste (about 3 ounces)

¼ cup sugar

3 eggs

4 tablespoons (½ stick) unsalted butter,
    at room temperature

⅓ cup all-purpose flour

1 can (15 ounces) apricot halves,
    drained, or 6 fresh apricots, halved
    and pitted

1 wedge (4 to 8 ounces) Manchego
    cheese

1 wedge (4 to 8 ounces) Monte Enebro
    cheese

1 wedge (4 to 8 ounces) Fourme
    d'Ambert cheese

To make the crust, in a large bowl, using an electric mixer, cream together the ½ cup butter and the sugar until the mixture is pale yellow. Add the egg and beat until the mixture is fluffy and light, stopping to scrape down the sides of the bowl with a rubber spatula as necessary. Add the flour and salt and mix well until the dough is fairly smooth.

Lightly flour a work surface and transfer the dough to the floured surface. Using the heel of your hand, spread the dough forward and then fold it back onto itself. Repeat five or six times until the dough is firm and smooth. Shape the dough into a ball and flatten lightly into a thick disk. Wrap the disk in plastic wrap and refrigerate for at least 2 hours or up to 2 days.

Preheat the oven to 350°F. Grease a 10-inch tart pan with a removable bottom with the remaining 1 tablespoon butter.

Lightly flour a work surface and transfer the dough to the floured surface. Using a rolling pin, roll out the dough into a circle about 12 inches in diameter. Carefully transfer the circle to the prepared pan, easing it into the bottom and sides and then lightly pressing it into place. Pinch the top edge to keep it even with the rim.

To make the filling, in a food processor, combine the almond paste and sugar and process until the mixture has a grainy consistency. Add the eggs, one at a time, processing after each addition until incorporated, then process until the mixture is smooth, about 1 minute. Add 2 tablespoons of the butter and mix for about 30 seconds. Add the remaining 2 tablespoons butter and mix for another 30 seconds to incorporate thoroughly. Using a rubber spatula, scrape the contents of the processor bowl into a large bowl. Sift the flour into the almond mixture, then, using the rubber spatula, stir the flour into the almond paste until fully blended.

Continue to use the rubber spatula to scrape the filling from the bowl into the crust, smoothing and leveling the surface. Place the apricot halves, upside down and evenly spaced, in a circle around the tart.

Bake the tart until the filling is firm and golden brown, about 30 minutes. Let cool on a wire rack for at least 1 hour. Remove the sides from the pan, then cut the tart into wedges and serve. Serve the cheeses on a platter. Invite diners to select a small portion of the cheese or cheeses that most interest them to accompany the tart.

SERVES 6

Cooper's Hawk Nightjar

The nightjar is a bird that makes its home in Portugal, the country that has inspired our American homage to Portugal's most renowned wine, Port. Cooper's Hawk Nightjar is a Port-style blend of several grape varieties: Touriga Nacional (considered to be the finest red grape in Portugal), Petite Sirah, and Cabernet Sauvignon. The wine is dark, dense, sweet, and rich. It is soft textured and packed with chocolate, spice, blackberries, and coffee flavors, perfect for a cheese course or a dessert, or both together, as featured here in Larry Binstein's Apricot-Almond Tart with Three Cheeses.

BASIC RECIPES

A number of recipes included in this book require ingredients that can be easily prepared at home, such as toasted nuts or roasted red peppers. Because they appear in multiple recipes, we have included them in this special section for ease of reference.

Of course, you can also use these recipes to spruce up all kinds of meals. For example, toasted nuts and seeds can add crunch to salads, candied walnuts are a great predinner nibble, or roasted red peppers drizzled with olive oil and sprinkled with sea salt make an excellent first course on their own. And the recipe for homemade mayonnaise is quite simple to prepare. Once you've mastered it, you may never make a sandwich with commercial mayonnaise again!

TOASTED NUTS AND SEEDS

Toasting nuts or seeds brings out their aroma and adds a welcome crunchiness. The technique requires nothing more than a small skillet or sauté pan and a stove top. But you'll need to remain alert to prevent burning. This can happen quite suddenly once you've achieved the desired toast.

In a small, dry skillet, toast the nuts or seeds over medium heat, stirring fairly constantly, until they are fragrant and have taken on color, then immediately pour onto a plate. Most seeds and nuts will be ready in 3 to 4 minutes. Larger nuts, such as hazelnuts or almonds, may require up to 8 to 10 minutes.

HOMEMADE MAYONNAISE

Unlike commercial mayonnaise, homemade mayonnaise is made without sugar or other sweeteners. It's easy to prepare and much creamier than

store-bought. For the best results, bring the egg yolk to room temperature before whisking.

1 egg yolk, at room temperature
1 teaspoon Dijon mustard
Pinch of salt
½ cup extra virgin olive oil
½ cup canola oil
1 clove garlic, minced

In a small to medium bowl, whisk together the egg yolk, mustard, and salt. Combine the oils in a measuring cup with a spout. While whisking constantly, add the oils to the yolk mixture, a few drops at a time, just until the mixture emulsifies. Once the mixture begins to emulsify, you can begin adding the oils a little more quickly, in a thin, steady stream. (To keep the bowl from moving around as you whisk, set it on a coiled kitchen towel.) Alternatively, in a food processor or blender, combine the yolk, mustard, garlic, and salt and pulse to mix. With the machine running, add the oils in a fine, steady stream, processing just until an emulsified sauce forms. Taste and add more salt if needed.

Cover and store in the refrigerator for up to 2 days.

MAKES ABOUT 1½ CUPS

ROASTED RED PEPPERS

These peppers are called for in a number of recipes in this book, including Three-Cheese Pizza with Roasted Red Peppers, Prosciutto, and Candied Walnuts (page 105); Linguine ai Frutti di Mare (page 93); Fried Catfish with Lemon-Jalapeño Coleslaw and Red Pepper Tartar Sauce (page 112); and Pork Tacos with Grilled Pineapple Salsa and Chile de Árbol (page 143). But you can also serve them on their own as a first course, dressed with a little extra virgin olive oil and salt.

Whether you roast 2 peppers or 10 peppers, the method is the same. Just remember that 2 raw peppers will yield about 1 cup roasted, seeded peppers. Store the peeled peppers in a plastic container in the refrigerator for up to 1 week. If peeled and immersed in olive oil, they will last for up to 2 weeks.

Preheat the oven to 400°F.

Arrange the peppers in a single layer on a rimmed baking sheet, roasting pan, or baking dish. Roast until the tops of the peppers begin to change color from red to black, 20 to 30 minutes. Remove from the oven and let cool.

Peel off the skins and remove the seeds by partially pulling the peppers apart under cold running water, using your fingers to rub the seeds away. Pull the peppers lengthwise into quarters or halves, discarding the stems, and pat them dry with paper towels. Use at once or store as described above.

MARY'S MASHED POTATOES

My mom has been making these potatoes since I was a child. When we opened the Orland Park restaurant, I had her bring pans of them over for the kitchen staff to try for three weeks in a row, until they finally mastered her recipe. Now our guests are able to enjoy what I have eaten for decades.

1½ pounds small red potatoes
1 pound Yukon Gold or other yellow-fleshed potatoes
4 tablespoons (½ stick) unsalted butter
¼ cup extra virgin olive oil
½ cup heavy cream, plus more if needed (optional)
1 teaspoon salt
Freshly ground black pepper

Cut the unpeeled potatoes into quarters or eighths, depending on their size. Fill a large pot two-thirds full with water and bring to a boil over high heat. Add the potatoes and cook until tender, about 20 minutes. (If the water threatens to boil over, lower the heat to medium-high.)

Drain the potatoes in a colander and shake dry, then return them to the pot. Add the butter and olive oil and, using a potato masher, mash the potatoes until they are "lumpy" smooth, about 30 seconds. Add the ½ cup cream and stir with a wooden spoon until the potatoes are creamy. If you want them softer and creamier, add additional cream. (It's okay if some lumps remain.)

Season with the salt and with pepper to taste and serve right away. Or, cover the pot and set aside; they will remain warm for up to about 15 minutes. You may also reheat them over medium heat, stirring occasionally, for about 1 minute.

SERVES 6

BETTY'S POTATOES

The first time I ate these potatoes was when Dana and I were dating and I was invited to her parents' house for dinner. I was a fan immediately. My mother-in-law, Betty, serves this dish at most family holiday meals. When we opened the first restaurant, I knew they had to be on the menu.

1 package (14 to 16 ounces) frozen hash brown potatoes, thawed
6 tablespoons (¾ stick) unsalted butter, melted
½ cup sour cream
¼ cup thinly sliced green onions, white and tender green parts only
1¾ cups shredded white Cheddar cheese
½ teaspoon kosher salt
⅛ teaspoon ground white pepper
1 can (10¾ ounces) Campbell's Condensed Cream of Chicken Soup
¼ cup panko (Japanese bread crumbs)

Preheat the oven to 350°F.

In a large bowl, combine the hash browns, 4 tablespoons of the melted butter, the sour cream, the green onions, 1 cup of the cheese, the salt, and the pepper. Open the soup can, add half of its contents to the bowl, and reserve the remainder for another use. Mix the ingredients well, then transfer the mixture to a baking dish. Top evenly with the remaining ¾ cup cheese.

In small bowl, stir together the bread crumbs and the remaining 2 tablespoons butter and sprinkle the mixture evenly over the cheese. Cover the baking dish. Bake for 40 minutes. Uncover and continue to bake until the top is crispy and golden brown, 3 to 5 minutes longer. Serve at once.

SERVES 6

CANDIED WALNUTS

These walnuts grace the top of Cooper's Hawk winemaker Rob Warren's three-cheese pizza (page 105). But you can also enjoy them as a snack, in salads, or as a crunchy treat alongside many Cooper's Hawk wines.

2 tablespoons unsalted butter
2 teaspoons firmly packed brown sugar
1 tablespoon maple sugar
Pinch of salt
2 cups walnut halves

Preheat the oven to 325°F.

In a small saucepan, melt the butter over low heat. Stir in the brown sugar, maple sugar, and salt, mixing well. Stir in the walnuts until they are evenly coated with the butter mixture.

Spread the walnuts on a rimmed baking sheet. Bake the nuts, stirring every 5 minutes to keep them from sticking and burning, until browned, about 15 minutes. Remove from the oven and let cool completely. Store in an airtight container in the refrigerator for up to 3 days.

MAKES 2 CUPS

INDEX

The Cooper's Hawk staff

ACKNOWLEDGMENTS

This book was conceived as a gift for our wine club members to say Thank You. First, I would like to express my gratitude to everyone who works at Cooper's Hawk Winery and Restaurants. Without them there would be no story to tell.

Over the years I've been blessed with many people who have believed in me and Cooper's Hawk from the start. In particular Richard and Andrea Gibb who supported me early on. I'd also like to thank the great team at Lynfred winery where I worked before opening Cooper's Hawk. I learned so much from owners Fred and Valerie as well and especially general manager, winemaker, and my friend Andrés Basso and his family.

As for the book team, many thanks go to Cooper's Hawk Director of Brand and Wine Club Development, Cathy Lowery, who coordinated the whole project from the very beginning. Book packager Leslie Jonath of Connected Dots Media put together a stellar team beginning with master writer/winemaker Jeff Morgan and terrific recipe tester and organizer, Jodie Morgan. We were delighted with Stephen Hamilton's beautiful photography expertly guided by art director and designer Shawn Hazen. We also appreciated the meticulous project management skills of Lisa McGuinness, who helped keep us on track with the help of Ursula Korus, our Coordinator of Wine Club and Restaurant Marketing. Thanks, too, to Jane Chinn for her print production expertise. Cooper's Hawk Chef, Matt McMillin, helped define the recipe strategy and contributed some recipes of his own. And Cooper's Hawk Winemaker Rob Warren was equally helpful, especially in introducing our wines and winery to Jeff Morgan. And of course, my sincere gratitude goes to the many chefs, and food and wine professionals who shared their recipes and passion with us. They are truly great friends of Cooper's Hawk, and I look forward to spending time with them for many years to come at special events in the winery and restaurants.

I want to thank my family, especially my patient and loving wife Dana, who is always there when I need her; my mother, Mary McEnery, who has always believed in me; my father Len and his wife, Lyn, for motivating me to be the best; John and Betty Cotte along with Mary Sloan for their constant support and encouragement; my grandparents, from whom my work ethic and obsession probably stems; and our amazing kids, who make it all worthwhile. Finally, I would like to express my sincerest gratitude to all of our Cooper's Hawk Wine Club members and guests. They are the ones who inspire us to do our best every day in our wineries, kitchens, dining, and tasting rooms.

Tim McEnery
Founder and CEO
Cooper's Hawk Winery and Restaurants